tearfund

8100 E. Arapahoe Rd., Suite #306, Centennial, CO 80112

To purchase copies, visit www.livejust.ly, or for bulk order, contact the publisher:

Tearfund USA
8100 E Arapahoe Rd, Suite #306
Centennial, CO 80112

1.888.789.4660
www.tearfundusa.org
www.livejust.ly

Contributors: Jason Fileta, Naomi Foxwood, Sunia Gibbs, Kimberly Hunt, René Padilla, Ronald J. Sider; José Marcos da Silva, Gaston Slanwa, Ashley Walker, Mari Williams and Nicholas Wolterstorff

Table of Contents

Introduction

We need to do justice to the concept of *"doing justice."*

Live Justly was first released in 2014. The resource has been used widely by churches and small groups, and has inspired people to live differently—to live justly. Tearfund USA brings you this exciting new edition of Live Justly. With contributors from Brazil, Sierra Leone, Ecuador, Sri Lanka, the UK, and the US, this work reflects global perspectives on what it means to live justly. We've reimagined the content for today's world listening to the Spirit to continue to discern the sacred work of mobilizing the Church to overcome poverty and injustice.

Tearfund has worked in partnership with the local church to overcome poverty and injustice for over 50 years. In that time we've learned that "doing justice" is much greater than a simple action—joining a campaign, signing a petition, or making a donation. We are called to not simply do justice, but to live justly. We want to do justice to the concept of "doing justice" by highlighting the deep and sacred nature of this calling.

Justice is often passionately invoked by teachers, pastors, and leaders inviting us into some kind of new action. For example, a pastor may preach on justice to encourage church members to volunteer or give to a project. Justice in these contexts is often focused upon doing something new, but what about the actions you and I already take every day? The difficult reality to accept is that so many of the seemingly benign decisions presented to us each and every day perpetuate injustice against God's children and creation. We must confront the world as it is with the world as it should be.

The work of justice has been cheapened by a culture obsessed with likes, clicks, and retweets. If we are not careful we can lull ourselves into a stupor of faux "righteousness" with every click, retweet, and call-out feeling satisfied as if we've done something for the Kingdom, when in fact all we've done is shown how clever we are. The work of justice is long suffering. It is filled with joy as we inevitably crash into God's grace over and over. It is love in action. It is sacred. It can't be satisfied simply through our tweets and musings.

We cannot begin to dismantle the systems that have created and perpetuated injustice simply by doing what we've always done—we need to embrace the imagination of the prophets, the faith of the disciples, and the radical love of Christ to reimagine our world without injustice. The world as it will be when Jesus reigns. When Jesus reigns there will be no more racism, sexism, abuse, environmental degradation, hunger, conflict, violence, or poverty. Justice is a central piece of God's redemption of this world—Christ is our salvation, and is our foundation for living justly

We are excited to go on this journey with you! We pray this resource inspires you, challenges you, and equips you to pray daily with your feet, hands and heart: "Your Kingdom come, your will be done on earth as it is in heaven."

Principles

Live Justly is a series of in-depth scriptural and practical studies to help people live justly in six key areas of life: prayer, advocacy, consumption, generosity, relationships, and creation care.

Live Justly was written on these core principles:

- Justice is part of the character and nature of God, and to live justly we must encounter God in a personal and powerful way;

- The Holy Spirit is our guide and our comfort;

- God works mightily through our relationships with one another, so *Live Justly* is designed to create a culture and community among participants that enable honest, convicting, and hope-filled discussion about justice;

- We will not reduce justice to a singular activity or marketing hook, thus perpetuating the false narrative that any of us are "saviors" of this world;

- We will not exploit people living in oppression and poverty for the sake of inspiring action;

- We cannot ask our leaders to practice things we are not willing to do ourselves. With this in mind, *Live Justly* is both inwardly and outwardly focused.

How To Use this Book

These studies are designed to help you and those in your community in your pursuit of justice from a place that is grounded in Scripture—whether that's at church, in work, or elsewhere—both in understanding and in practice. The goal is to come out of the ten sessions with:

- Deepened relationships with your small group;

- A deep understanding of justice rooted in scripture;

- Passion and inspiration for action;

- An individual action plan that shows what practical steps you will take, or shifts you will make, to live justly. (this is shared with your small group in Session 10);

- A collective action plan to mobilize your church or community for justice.

In addition to the ten studies we have included information to help you develop a baseline understanding of some of the most critical injustices of our time—these will be helpful resources on your own and your community's journey toward living justly.

Each session includes:

- **Definitions** - to make sure everyone has the same knowledge base;
- **Story** - a short, provoking story or reflection to help you see that session's topic played out in real life;
- **Essay** - a deeper reflection on the session's topic (this is a great source for your group discussion);
- **Scripture** - to examine what the Bible has to say on that session's topic (we encourage you to read the scripture out loud as a group!);
- **Questions** to help you generate a lively discussion;
- **Activities** that we call "Together" for you to do as a group to help understand and explore the concepts further;
- **Solo work** - light homework to help you process the small group time, reflect, pray, and slowly develop an action-plan;
- **Those with good internet access can find additional resources online at www.livejust.ly.**

Sample small group session:

1. Welcome and introduction
2. Ask if anyone is willing to give a summary of the reading, or highlight the portions that stood out to them. Group leader can also provide a summary of the main themes.
3. Read that sessions Scripture passage out loud
4. Engage in discussion about the story, scripture and essay for that session—feel free to use the questions or generate your own
5. Together activity
6. Prayer and close

A Word About the Logo

The Live Justly logo is a visual representation of our framework for living justly:

- Each side of the hexagon represents one facet of life in which you will be equipped to live justly: prayer, advocacy, consumption, generosity, relationships, and creation care. The circle represents the holistic nature of living justly. If we are incredible advocates, but do so at the expense of our personal relationships, then we can focus on growing in relationships. If we are compassionate to those who are poor, but fail to challenge unjust structures that cause their oppression, then we can focus on growing in advocacy. The circle represents a holistic, unified lifestyle pointed towards justice.

- The fire symbolizes our posture of worship. The journey toward justice is not meant to be pursued as a list to tick off, but a lifestyle to embrace and embolden us towards kingdom living. Justice is part of the character and nature of God. So every decision we make for the kingdom of God, whether small or large, is an act of worship

- The bread symbolizes the essential need for community. We cannot live justly without pursuing meaningful, accountable, authentic community. The circle will break if it is not held together by many hands.

Let's Do This

The content of this book will not give you a prescription for living justly, but our prayer is that you will encounter God, be influenced by the Holy Spirit, sharpen your passions, and find community that spurs you to renewed action. We are excited and honored to journey with you to live justly!

Part One

Foundations

What is Biblical Justice? A theology of justice

"There is a long and venerable Christian tradition that speaks of justice for the poor. Justice has to do with rights. Justice is present in social relationships insofar as people are enjoying what they have a right to. When people do not enjoy those goods to which they have a right, they are wronged. And these rights stem from the intrinsic worth of men and women created in the image of God and provided for bountifully out of his fertile earth. Jesus and the biblical prophets did not think of rendering assistance to the needy of the world in terms of charity but in terms of justice." Vinoth Ramachandra

"Part of living justly is recognizing that the decisions we make affect not only the people around us but communities and environments around the world. We must live our lives and make choices with that in mind." Kimberly Hunt

Definitions

Biblical Justice: Action taken to restore flourishing and wholeness. "Biblical" refers to the concept of justice in scripture's teachings.

Shalom: Hebrew word for peace, completeness, and wholeness. Where there is justice, there will be shalom.

Year of Jubilee: Every fifty years, the Israelites were to partake in a year of celebration and liberation. They would restore lands, property and property rights to original owners, debts were cancelled, and slaves were set free.

Doing Justice Is Never That Simple

There was a church in the United States that annually went on a short-term mission trip to Sierra Leone in West Africa. Over the years, over 100 short termers built meaningful and deeply authentic relationships with Sierra Leonean Christians—worshipping alongside them, painting the church building side by side, beautifying local schools together, and distributing food and toys to children together. They spent years building not only relationships but also wells and walls.

As the years went on, the community in and around the Sierra Leonean church experienced an increase in devastating floods, landslides, hunger, and poverty. It was becoming more difficult to grow crops in a changing climate. Irregular rains made the soil dry and hard, making traditional crops nearly impossible to grow without irrigation or fertilizer, and when it did rain, it rained so hard that it quickly washed out crops, land and homes. Climate change was devastating their community.

The US church noticed the increased levels of hunger and poverty, as well as the destruction of the very wells and walls they had built. They responded by launching a giving appeal in their church—a campaign to raise funds to help build new homes and new wells. In addition, they found a local ministry to partner with to package nutrient-rich dehydrated meals and ship them to their friends in Sierra Leone. The church truly stepped up—the hundreds of short termers mobilized hundreds more volunteers to pack meal after meal for their brothers and sisters in Sierra Leone.

In a phone call between the pastors of the two churches, the Sierra Leonean pastor thanked his counterpart in the US for the funds raised and for the food, but he lamented the unknown future he and his community faced. He lamented how little politicians in countries like the US were doing to combat climate change, and how communities like his were suffering despite having done next to nothing to contribute to climate change. The American pastor was shocked and hurt that his dear friend was making things political, in fact, his

friend almost seemed ungrateful. Why couldn't his friend just celebrate these gifts of generosity and love? They had provided a solution—God had provided a solution. What did climate change have to do with any of this?

For people experiencing hunger, an endless supply of dehydrated food is not providing justice—it is a band-aid solution, and as we all know, band aids are intended to stop the immediate flow of blood, and then fall off after a day. If the solution to injustice seems simple, it's likely not a solution at all.

God Loves Justice,
by Nicholas Wolterstorff

What the Hebrew and Christian scriptures have to say about justice functions for many people nowadays mainly as a source of golden nuggets of rhetoric - if it functions for them at all. Who could improve on the following if one is urging the importance of doing justice:

"Away with the noise of your songs! I will not listen to the music of your harps. But let justice roll on like a river, righteousness like a never-failing stream!" Amos 5:23-24

or this:

"He has shown you, O mortal, what is good. And what does the Lord require of you? To act justly and

to love mercy and to walk humbly with your God."
Micah 6:8

What scripture says about justice is more than "nuggets" of wisdom. There is a clear way of thinking about justice in the scriptures – and what those writings say about justice is an inextricable component of the message. Pull out justice, and everything unravels.

Some of the skeptics of justice in scripture are secularists who have gotten the impression that Christianity is all about love and not about justice. But a good many are Christians who have not so much gotten the impression that Christianity is all about love and not about justice, but are committed to interpreting scripture solely through the lens of love. And then there are those who concede that scripture speaks of justice but assume that it refers to kings and courts in the administration of justice. When I say that justice is an inextricable component of the biblical message, I have in mind primary justice.

There are two different kinds of justice in scripture: primary justice and reactive justice.

Reactive justice punishes the wrongdoer, condemns the wrongdoer, is perhaps angry at the wrongdoer, and so forth—reacting to one's wrongdoing. Reactive justice renders justice to a wrongdoer.

What that implies, obviously, is that reactive justice is relevant when someone has wronged someone else, when someone has treated another person unjustly. And what that implies, in turn, is that reactive justice cannot be the only kind of justice. There has to be another kind of justice—a kind of justice such that, when someone violates this other kind of justice, and is thus a wrongdoer, reactive justice becomes relevant.

I am going to call it primary justice. Reactive justice becomes relevant when there has been a violation of primary justice.

God loves primary justice. God has a heart for primary justice. God is devoted to justice. So it comes as no surprise that God says: "Seek justice; do justice; let justice roll down like waters; imitate me in loving justice." But is God speaking of reactive justice, reserved for courts, kings, and judges, or primary justice, which applies to all people? I believe that, in many cases, these scriptures are speaking of primary justice.

MISHPAT & TSEDEQA

The Hebrew word in the Old Testament that is usually translated into English as justice is "misphat." The term is often paired with "tsedeqa," standardly translated as "righteousness." Together they are often translated as "justice and righteousness" in the Old Testament and simply "righteousness" in the New Testament. My own sense is that, when the rhetorical context permits, "tsedeqa" is better rendered into present-day English as the right thing, going right, or doing right. The word righteous is almost never used any more in ordinary speech, and when it is, it suggests a person intensely preoccupied with his own moral character who has few sins to his debit. The connotation is self-righteousness. The pairing of "mishpat" and "tsedeqa" is better translated as primary justice or simply "justice" than as "justice and righteousness" or simply "righteousness."

Scripture teaches that what God wants for God's human family is what the Old Testament writers called, in Hebrew, shalom. "Shalom" is almost always translated as "peace" in our English bibles. I think that is a very poor translation. Shalom is much more than peace. Shalom is flourishing. What God desires for us is that we flourish in all dimensions of our existence.

And now for the point relevant to our purposes here: when you read what the biblical writers say about shalom, it soon becomes clear that shalom requires justice. In the absence of justice, we are not truly flourishing; in the absence of justice, shalom is impaired. Shalom goes beyond justice, but shalom always includes justice. Justice is, you might say, the ground floor of shalom. So once again: why does God love justice? Because God loves shalom, and shalom includes justice.

When the kingdom of God has come in its fullness, there will be no breaches of primary justice, and hence no reactive justice; all justice will be primary justice. You and I are to imitate God by also having a heart for justice.

Read Isaiah 61: The Year of the Lord's Favor

Isaiah 61

1 The Spirit of the Sovereign Lord is on me, because the Lord has anointed me to proclaim good news to the poor. He has sent me to bind up the brokenhearted, to proclaim freedom for the captives and release from darkness for the prisoners,

2 to proclaim the year of the Lord's favor and the day of vengeance of our God, to comfort all who mourn,

3 and provide for those who grieve in Zion - to bestow on them a crown of beauty instead of ashes, the oil of joy instead of mourning, and a garment of praise instead of a spirit of despair. They will be called oaks of righteousness, a planting of the Lord for the display of his splendor.

4 They will rebuild the ancient ruins and restore the places long devastated; they will renew the ruined cities that have been devastated for generations.

5 Strangers will shepherd your flocks; foreigners will work your fields and vineyards.

6 And you will be called priests of the Lord, you will be named ministers of our God. You will feed on the wealth of nations, and in their riches you will boast.

7 Instead of your shame you will receive a double portion, and instead of disgrace you will rejoice in your inheritance. And so you will inherit a double portion in your land, and everlasting joy will be yours.

8 "For I, the Lord, love justice; I hate robbery and wrongdoing. In my faithfulness I will reward my people and make an everlasting covenant with them.

9 Their descendants will be known among the nations and their offspring among the peoples. All who see them will acknowledge that they are a people the Lord has blessed."

10 I delight greatly in the Lord; my soul rejoices in my God. For he has clothed me with garments of salvation and arrayed me in a robe of his righteousness, as a bridegroom adorns his head like a priest, and as a bride adorns herself with her jewels.

11 For as the soil makes the sprout come up and a garden causes seeds to grow, so the Sovereign Lord will make righteousness and praise spring up before all nations.

Questions for Discussion

1. What is justice?

_____

_____

_____

2. Why do you think Jesus quoted this passage in his first sermon (Luke 4:18)?

_____

_____

_____

3. In the absence of the year of Jubilee, how do we ensure a "reset" to undo the structural and personal sin that perpetuates oppression?

_____

_____

_____

4. What is God saying to you, and what are you going to do about it?

_____

_____

_____

Together

How have you viewed the concept of justice? Most often, people tend to think of justice in a retributive sense—for example, the criminal justice system. Using the reading from this week and the discussion you had, consider your own group's definition of justice. Be sure to allow everyone to contribute.

Solo Work

Read Luke 4:16-21. With a knowledge of Jesus' work displayed in the Gospels, and the context of God's desire for justice detailed in Isaiah 61, explain Jesus' words, "Today this scripture is fulfilled in your hearing."

- How does Jesus' work on earth fulfill the teachings of Isaiah 61?

_____

_____

_____

- How is this session's message and discussion challenging you? Are you one who knows God, but has resisted justice? Are you much more comfortable with justice but have resisted God?

_____

_____

_____

Journal about this. Be vulnerable. Be open. This is between you and God.

Prayer

Lord, you know my heart. If I have claimed to know you, but have resisted seeking justice, forgive me. If I have passionately sought justice but have been detached from you, draw me near to you. Help me recognize your Spirit in me and respond to your call to seek justice.

Our Mission in the World: Integral mission

"If we ignore the world, we betray the word of God which sends us out to serve the world. If we ignore the word of God, we have nothing to bring to the world." The Micah Declaration on Integral Mission[1]

"The risen Jesus expects that his disciple-community, which is preaching the Good News among the nations, is also striving at Christian unity, is sharing its resources with the poor and needy, is engaged in costly initiatives of peacemaking, and hungering and thirsting after God's justice." Vinoth Ramachandra

Definitions

Integral Mission: Integral mission is the church speaking of and living out its faith in Jesus Christ in every aspect of life. Integral mission is the work of the church in contributing to the positive physical, spiritual, economic, psychological, and social transformation of people.

Kingdom of God: The place where Jesus reigns and shalom is reality. All things are made right. The kingdom is already here, but not in fullness. We only see glimpses and tastes of the kingdom until Christ's return.

The Body vs. the Soul

I have often met people who respond to a sermon or a teaching of mine by extolling the virtue of my work to end poverty, but often ask, "Do you preach the Gospel as well?" It's a more polite version of what a confrontational pastor told me a few years back: "What good is it to feed the hungry if when they die they simply go to hell? If you truly love someone you'll want to get to eternity with God—that matters more than feeding them." I understand this sentiment—it is a temptation for both the privileged and the oppressed to adopt this thinking. For the former, it is an easy way to justify their lifestyles, priorities, and often, politics; for the latter, it is comforting to find something to hope for amidst immense pain and suffering. A better question to ask is: If we preach the Gospel and make disciples, but nothing about society changes, have we preached the Gospel of Jesus Christ? Or more simply put: If the "good news" isn't good news to the poor, then is it the good news of Jesus Christ?

This false choice between saving the body vs. saving the soul assumes that becoming a disciple of Christ is completely compatible with the economics, cultures, and politics of this world. It assumes that following Jesus is a perfectly personal journey that will impact nothing about how we live other than personal holiness. We need

[1] Read the entire Micah Declaration on Integral Mission on page 77

not look any further than the life of Jesus and the early church to realize this is an absolutely unbiblical approach. If our proclamation of Jesus doesn't upset the culture around us (and no, I'm not referring to the great secular CD smashings of the 1990s) in order to give bread to those who are hungry, break the chains of injustice, and set the oppressed free, then we must consider whether we are proclaiming Jesus of Nazareth or simply a construct we've made that resembles him.

The good news is that Jesus has redeemed ALL THINGS—my soul and yours, but also the brokenness reaped by sin in our world—hunger, racism, persecution, and violence. All will be restored by Christ. So our mission in the world must reflect the fullness of his salvation—healing for the body and soul.

Integral Mission,
by René Padilla

Although it has recently become fashionable to use the term integral mission, the approach to mission that it expresses is not new. The practice of integral mission goes back to Jesus himself and to the first-century Christian church. Furthermore, a growing number of churches are putting this style of mission into practice without necessarily using this expression to refer to what they are doing; integral mission is not part of their vocabulary. It is clear that the practice of integral mission is much more important than the use of this new expression to refer to it.

The expression integral mission (misión integral) came into use principally within the Latin American Theological Fraternity (FTL) about twenty years ago. It was an attempt to highlight the importance of conceiving the mission of the church within a more biblical theological framework than the traditional one, which had been accepted in evangelical circles due to the influence of the modern missionary movement. What is this approach to mission? In what aspects does it differ from the traditional transcultural approach?

INTEGRAL MISSION, A NEW PARADIGM

From the perspective of integral mission, traditional transcultural mission is far from exhausting the significance of the mission of the church. Mission may or may not include a crossing of geographical frontiers, but in every case it means primarily a crossing of the frontier between faith and no faith, whether in one's own country (at home) or in a foreign country (on the mission field), according to the testimony to Jesus Christ as Lord of the whole of life and of the whole creation. Let's examine four key differences between integral mission and traditional transcultural mission.

INTEGRAL MISSION

All churches send and all churches receive. The road of mission is not a one-way street. It does not go only from the Christian countries to the pagan countries; it is a two-way street.

The whole world is a mission field, and every human need is an opportunity for missionary service. The local church is called to demonstrate the reality of the kingdom of God among the kingdoms of this world, not only by what it says, but also by what it is and by what it does in response to human needs on every side.

Every Christian is called to follow Jesus Christ and to be committed to God's mission in the world. The benefits of salvation are inseparable from a missionary lifestyle, and this implies, among other things, the practice of the universal priesthood of believers in all spheres of human life, according to the gifts and ministries that the Spirit of God has freely bestowed on his people.

The Christian life in all its dimensions, on both the individual and the community levels, is the primary witness to the universal lordship of Jesus Christ and the transforming power of the Holy Spirit. Mission is much more than words; it is demonstrated in the life that recovers God's original purpose for the relationship of the human person with his Creator, with his neighbor, and with all of creation.

TRADITIONAL TRANSCULTURAL MISSION

Some churches send, almost exclusively from Western Christianity, and some churches receive, almost exclusively from the Global South.

Only the receiving country is viewed as a mission field. The missionaries "home" is usually somewhere in the Christian West, and their "mission field" is located in some pagan country. It is not surprising that the majority of career missionaries (sometimes with years of service) decide to retire in their home country.

Only some Christians are missionaries. There are missionaries, called by God to serve him, and then there are common ordinary Christians, who enjoy the benefits of salvation but are exempt from sharing in what God wants to do in the world.

The life of the church and the mission of the church could be separated. If, in order for a church to be a missionary church, it were sufficient to send and support a few of its members to serve in foreign missions, it is possible that such a church would have no significant influence or impact on its surrounding neighborhood: the life of the church is local (at home), and mission takes place in another setting, preferably in a foreign country (the mission field).

When the church is committed to integral mission and to communicating the gospel through everything it is, does, and says, it understands that its goal is not to become large numerically, nor to be rich materially, nor powerful politically. Its purpose is to incarnate the values of the kingdom of God and to witness to the love and the justice revealed in Jesus Christ, by the power of the Spirit, for the transformation of human life in all its dimensions, both on the individual level and on the community level.

The accomplishment of this purpose presupposes that all the members of the church, without exception, by the very fact of having become a part of the Body of Christ, receive gifts and ministries for the exercise of their priesthood, to which they have been ordained in their baptism. Mission is not the responsibility and privilege of a small group of the faithful who feel called to the mission field (usually in a foreign country), but of all members, since all are members of the royal priesthood and as such have been called by God that they may declare the praises of him who called them out of darkness into his wonderful light (1 Peter 2:9), wherever they may be.

Understood in these terms, this new paradigm for mission is not so new; it is, rather, the recovery of the biblical concept of mission since, in effect, mission is faithful to the teaching of scripture to the extent that it is placed at the service of the kingdom of God and his justice.

Integral mission is the means designed by God to carry out, within history, his purpose of love and justice revealed in Jesus Christ, through the church and in the power of the Spirit.

Read Matthew 22:34-40 Together

The Greatest Commandment

34 Hearing that Jesus had silenced the Sadducees, the Pharisees got together.

35 One of them, an expert in the law, tested him with this question:

36 "Teacher, which is the greatest commandment in the Law?"

37 Jesus replied: "'Love the Lord your God with all your heart and with all your soul and with all your mind.'

38 This is the first and greatest commandment.

39 And the second is like it: 'Love your neighbor as yourself.'

40 All the Law and the Prophets hang on these two commandments."

Read Matthew 28:16-20
Together

The Great Commission

16 Then the eleven disciples went to Galilee, to the mountain where Jesus had told them to go. 17 When they saw him, they worshiped him; but some doubted.

18 Then Jesus came to them and said, "All authority in heaven and on earth has been given to me.

19 Therefore go and make disciples of all nations, baptizing them in the name of the Father and of the Son and of the Holy Spirit,

20 and teaching them to obey everything I have commanded you. And surely I am with you always, to the very end of the age."

Questions for Discussion

1. According to an integral mission framework, any work of the church to usher in the kingdom of God is mission. Do you agree with this? What activities become "missions" that have not typically been identified as such?

    _____

    _____

    _____

2. Can we fulfill the great commission without seeking justice? Why, or why not?

    _____

    _____

    _____

3. Has preaching/teaching on the great commission ever compelled you to pursue justice?

    _____

    _____

    _____

4. What is God saying to you, and what are you going to do about it?

    _____

    _____

    _____

Together

On a piece of paper, make two columns with the headings "Integral Mission" and "Disconnected Mission." Describe your own experiences with missions—church, university or school missions, short-term mission trips, mission weeks, etc.—and write down your name and the experience under the column where your mission work would fall. Does your group have more experiences in one column or another? Discuss those activities that fell under the "disconnected missions." List the ways you could reshape those activities to be more integral.

Solo Work

Begin to work on a creative expression of your understanding of justice and any story, issue, or scripture that impacts your understanding of justice. This might include poetry, spoken word, visual art (painting, drawing, photography), short stories, and anything else that makes your creativity come alive! You will continue to work on this creative expression each week and you will have an opportunity to share with one another in Session Ten (if you desire).

Prayer

Lord, make me an instrument of your kingdom. Help me to be missional even when it is uncomfortable. Help me to challenge the economic, political, and social systems of our world that are in need of redemption. Help me to bravely proclaim the gospel to my neighbors, near and far, and may many come to know and follow you.

Justice in Action: From charity to advocacy

"We are not to simply bandage the wounds of victims beneath the wheels of injustice, we are to drive a spoke into the wheel itself." Dietrich Bonhoeffer

"Charity is no substitute for justice withheld." St. Augustine

Definitions

Relief: Assistance, generally one-time or short-term, in the form of food, clothing, or money offered to people in crisis.

Charity: A voluntary act or gift contributed to those in need, given out of compassion or love.

Structural Injustice: Sin that infects the systems that govern society such as economic and political systems.

Saint or Communist?

"When I give food to the poor, they call me a saint. When I ask why they are poor, they call me a communist." Archbishop Hélder Pessoa Câmara

Archbishop Hélder Pessoa Câmara was known for his work in the slums of Brazil, forming small groups of Brazilan peasants to read the Gospels, and then move to action opposing the military dictatorship that was ruling Brazil at the time. The urban poor of Brazil didn't have access to land or to capital—no banks would lend money to allow people to start businesses and try to lift themselves out of poverty.

Rather than simply organizing the Gospel reading groups and distributing food, the Archbishop founded a nonprofit bank focused on lending money to those deemed too high risk by traditional financial institutions. But his story doesn't end there—he spoke out, at great risk to himself, against the violence used by the state at the time. **What a beautiful and holistic response to poverty— and how rare it is to see.**

Too often, the anti-poverty and justice movements within the church have fractured along ideological lines—some are unwilling or unable to see the structural causes of injustice and poverty. They see sin, bad life choices, or harsh circumstances, but are unable to see unjust laws, exploitation, and systemic discrimination. On the other hand, some folks have become so enamored with the systemic that they disregard the value of charity—giving food to the hungry and water to the thirsty as if they were Christ (Matthew 25). What a different model we have in leaders from the Global South, like Archbishop Câmara—who practiced a holistic, gospel-centered approach to justice.

It is time to move beyond the paradigm of the prior generation—to embrace a holistic approach to injustice.

The Circle of Justice,
by Jason Fileta

A few years ago I spoke at a conference to inspire support for a piece of legislation called the Jubilee Act. Essentially, there were sixty-seven nations who were servicing debts to the US government at the expense of being able to provide healthcare, education, and water to their people. The debts they were repaying, some of them decades old, were often lent irresponsibly to dictators at very high interest rates, and we were punishing the citizens of these nations by requiring the repayment of this debt.

It was a justice issue. It was a justice issue that could only be resolved with effective and prophetic advocacy. We could try to set up hospitals, schools, and feeding programs in those sixty-seven nations, but the underlying cause of their inability to do it

themselves would still be there: their debt. My role was to inspire the attendees of this conference to not just look upon the hungry with compassion and give them bread, but to encourage them to ask why they were hungry—to take decisive action to fix an unjust policy.

After the conference was over, I and the other speakers went out for dinner. At dinner, I mentioned some of the things I had been struggling with at this conference and many other justice and advocacy conferences I had spoken at previously. I was struggling with the disconnectedness of our principles of justice and how we actually ran the conference. The voices of people living in poverty were often absent, food and other resources were often wasted, and the opportunities for generosity and charitable acts were few or none. However, the opportunities for advocacy were many, but our advocacy alone seemed incomplete.

One of the other speakers essentially told me I needed to relax and remember why I do what I do. She explained that she lived in a huge house, in a comfortable, safe neighborhood and indulged in a nice glass of wine and fine food because that was what she deserved, or what was needed to keep her going in the fight for justice. She implied that she (or me for that matter) didn't need to be radically generous, or consume less for the sake of giving more directly to those living in poverty because she was dealing with the structural causes of injustice. We didn't need to be bothered with small acts of charity.

Something didn't feel right.

Here is the reality. Advocacy is not justice. Charity is not justice. The picture of justice we see in scripture is a prerequisite for shalom—a time when all brokenness is made right. When relationships between people are healed, relationships between people and God are healed, relationships between people and systems are healed, relationships between people and creation are healed, and one's own relationship with self is healed. Advocacy and charity are certainly essential components of justice, and therefore shalom, but neither is a synonym for justice.

For so long we've seen people hungry, no matter how much we feed them. This has led a movement of us to work for an end to hunger not by delivering more food but by delivering more justice through advocating to governments and corporations for more just policies and practices. Let me tell you something - it is fun to be an advocate. Sometimes, it is exhilarating. To know that your work helped create a level playing field is incredible. To stand in the halls of power and speak prophetically is euphoric (and scary!). I imagine it is similar (although on a much smaller scale) to the exhilaration Moses felt leading the Israelites out of slavery in Egypt.

In fact, a lot of advocates (myself included) use the story of Moses and the exodus to highlight the essential role of advocacy. God called Moses to go to Pharaoh, the political leader of the day, and release the Israelites from slavery. He didn't call Moses to go to the Israelites and comfort, feed, and clothe them through setting up a charity, all the while not addressing the cause of their suffering. But does this mean God was not concerned about their immediate needs being met? Returning to the issue of hunger in our day, does this mean God is not concerned about the hungry being fed while we dismantle unjust policies that cause hunger?

Absolutely not!

The whole of scripture points to a God who wants to see the "captives released, the hungry fed and the naked clothed." Advocacy alone will not accomplish this. Neither will charity alone.

I am certain that though Moses' calling as an advocate was unique, there were others—perhaps thousands—called to radical acts of charity and generosity to clothe, comfort and feed the Israelites while still in slavery. It is only consistent with our God that he called up compassionate people to be His presence among the Israelites. Both callings were necessary, both are worthy, and both are part of the call to do justice.

Biblical justice is holistic in nature. It is a circle made up of many points. If we are tireless advocates, but at the expense of our personal relationships, then the circle is broken. If we are compassionate to the impoverished through charity and generosity, but fail to challenge unjust structures that cause their oppression, then, again, the circle is broken.

To truly see justice done we must become competent and committed to a holistic lifestyle of justice, including charity and advocacy. We must not choose one over the other, but rather recognize what our unique calling is while still embracing the other things God calls us to in a lifestyle of justice. Let the circle be unbroken!

Read Exodus 3 Together
Moses and the Burning Bush

1 Now Moses was tending the flock of Jethro his father-in-law, the priest of Midian, and he led the flock to the far side of the wilderness and came to Horeb, the mountain of God.

2 There the angel of the Lord appeared to him in flames of fire from within a bush. Moses saw that though the bush was on fire it did not burn up.

3 So Moses thought, "I will go over and see this strange sight - why the bush does not burn up." 4 When the Lord saw that he had gone over to look, God called to him from within the bush, "Moses! Moses!" And Moses said, "Here I am."

5 "Do not come any closer," God said. "Take off your sandals, for the place where you are standing is holy ground."

6 Then he said, "I am the God of your father, the God of Abraham, the God of Isaac and the God of Jacob." At this, Moses hid his face, because he was afraid to look at God.

7 The Lord said, "I have indeed seen the misery of my people in Egypt. I have heard them crying out because of their slave drivers, and I am concerned about their suffering.

8 So I have come down to rescue them from the hand of the Egyptians and to bring them up out of that land into a good and spacious land, a land flowing with milk and honey - the home of the Canaanites, Hittites, Amorites, Perizzites, Hivites and Jebusites.

9 And now the cry of the Israelites has reached me, and I have seen the way the Egyptians are oppressing them.

10 So now, go. I am sending you to Pharaoh to bring my people the Israelites out of Egypt."

11 But Moses said to God, "Who am I that I should go to Pharaoh and bring the Israelites out of Egypt?"

12 And God said, "I will be with you. And this will be the sign to you that it is I who have sent you: When you have brought the people out of Egypt, you will worship God on this mountain."

13 Moses said to God, "Suppose I go to the Israelites and say to them, 'The God of your fathers has sent me to you,' and they ask me, 'What is his name?' Then what shall I tell them?"

14 God said to Moses, "I am who I am. This is what you are to say to the Israelites: 'I am has sent me to you.'"

15 God also said to Moses, "Say to the Israelites, 'The Lord, the God of your fathers - the God of Abraham, the God of Isaac and the God of Jacob - has sent me to you.' "This is my name forever, the name you shall call me from generation to generation.

16 "Go, assemble the elders of Israel and say to them, 'The Lord, the God of your fathers - the God of Abraham, Isaac and Jacob - appeared to me and said: I have watched over you and have seen what has been done to you in Egypt.

17 And I have promised to bring you up out of your misery in Egypt into the land of the Canaanites, Hittites, Amorites, Perizzites, Hivites and Jebusites - a land flowing with milk and honey.'

18 The elders of Israel will listen to you. Then you and the elders are to go to the king of Egypt and say to him, 'The Lord, the God of the Hebrews, has met with us. Let us take a three-day journey into the wilderness to offer sacrifices to the Lord our God.'

19 But I know that the king of Egypt will not let you go unless a mighty hand compels him.

20 So I will stretch out my hand and strike the Egyptians with all the wonders that I will perform among them. After that, he will let you go.

21 And I will make the Egyptians favorably disposed toward this people, so that when you leave you will not go empty-handed.

22 Every woman is to ask her neighbor and any woman living in her house for articles of silver and gold and for clothing, which you will put on your sons and daughters. And so you will plunder the Egyptians.

Questions for Discussion

1. If Moses was called to help those in slavery today, what do you think the church would think of his strategy?

    _____

    _____

    _____

2. Can you think of an example of well-intentioned Christians trying to combat injustice through charity alone? Did it free people?

    _____

    _____

    _____

3. Consider the issue of hunger. In what ways can we respond to hunger, not just through providing food, but through loosening the chains of injustice?

    _____

    _____

    _____

4. What is God saying to you, and what are you going to do about it?

    _____

    _____

    _____

Together

As a group, choose one specific justice issue (e.g., racism, hunger, climate change). Brainstorm what engagement would look like if charity and advocacy united for justice.

Now consider your own engagement with a justice issue you are passionate about. Share which path you tend to gravitate toward: a response of charity, advocacy, or a mixture of both? How are you feeling challenged to engage with the issue you are passionate about in a new way?

Solo Work

Consider a justice issue facing your community. Identify the problem, and search for the root cause by continuing to ask, "Why?" Now consider the existing responses to the problem. Are they treating the symptoms, the root or both? Continue to work on your creative expression.

Prayer

Lord, give me eyes to see the structures and systems that perpetuate injustice. Help me also to see the immediate needs of the oppressed, and may I never seek justice at the expense of being charitable. Give me a courageous voice to hold my leaders accountable to how their decisions affect the vulnerable.

Part Two

Action

Justice and Prayer: Changing the world through prayer

"Prayer makes your heart bigger, until it is capable of containing the gift of God himself. Prayer begets faith, faith begets love, and love begets service on behalf of the poor." Mother Teresa

"We are to change the world through prayer." Richard J. Foster

"Intercessory prayer is spiritual defiance of what is in the way of what God has promised. Intercession visualizes an alternative future to the one apparently fated by the momentum of current forces. Prayer infuses the air of a time yet to be into the suffocating atmosphere of the present. History belongs to the intercessors who believe the future into being. Intercession, far from being an escape from action, is a means of focusing for action and of creating action. By means of our intercessions we veritably cast fire upon the earth and trumpet the future into being." Walter Wink

Definitions

Cupbearer: Nehemiah's role for King Artaxerxes. The position of cupbearer was one of the most trusted positions in the court, as the cupbearer was the one who tested and made sure that all of the king's food and drink weren't poisoned before he consumed them. As a result of this role, Nehemiah was in a place of great influence with the king.

We are tired of running

From 1989 to 2003, the Liberian civil war raged, leaving the country and its people absolutely devastated. Two to three hundred people were massacred daily, gang rape became commonplace, and people were constantly being displaced from their homes. One day, a woman named Leymah Gbowee had a strange dream of God telling her to "gather up the women and pray for peace."

And she did exactly what God called her to. She began with a handful of women in a fish market praying for peace. In a beautiful display of God's love, both Christian and Muslim women gathered in public places and sang and prayed for peace. They took sometimes unexpected, nonviolent actions such as organizing a sex strike, sit-ins, fasts, and takeovers of public places to sing, worship, and pray for peace. Their mantra rang out:

We are tired of war. We are tired of running. We are tired of begging for bulgur wheat. We are tired of our children being raped. We are now taking this stand to secure the future of our children because we believe, as custodians of society, tomorrow our children will ask us, "Mama, what was your role during the crisis?"

After several months, President Charles Taylor granted the women a hearing. They successfully urged him to attend peace talks in Ghana that would take place in June 2003.

Gbowee led the women to the peace talks in Ghana to ensure that progress was made. When she found that the leaders were not taking the process seriously, they sat down in the halls where the talks were taking place, essentially holding everyone in the room hostage until an agreement was definitively made. A settlement was reached, the peace agreement was signed, and in August 2003 the civil war officially ended—just one year after Leymah and the women of the fish market began praying passionately for peace.

Walter Wink describes the power of prayer to change our world in his book Engaging the Powers: "Intercessory prayer is spiritual defiance of what is in the way of what God has promised. Intercession visualizes an alternative future to the one apparently fated by the momentum of current forces. Prayer infuses the air of a time yet to be into the suffocating atmosphere of the present. **History belongs to the intercessors who believe the future into being**. Even a small number of people, firmly committed to the new inevitability on which they have fixed their imaginations, can decisively affect the shape the future takes."

May we all be courageous enough to pray as Leymah and her community did.

Passionate prayer for peace, *by Jason Fileta*

I've noticed that I often see prayer not as an action itself but as a predecessor to my "real" action. I think many of us do. We open meetings with prayer; we pray to kick off big events, but what about prayer as action? Prayers like Nehemiah's, like Leymah's in Liberia, that change the world? Prayer changes us, changes our world, and sustains us in the long and difficult struggle to live justly.

Many of us pray daily for our families and loved ones. We also send sporadic, urgent prayers in times of great need—when the challenges of life seem so overwhelming that we don't know what else to do. In seeking justice, this will always be the temptation. The challenges of hunger, gender equality, slavery, and extreme poverty are all much bigger than we can manage. What if we prayed faithfully as Nehemiah or as Leymah for an end to hunger? For an end to slavery? What if we prayed with the same fervor for our brothers and sisters in extreme poverty as we would for our own children?

I have no doubt that these prayers would not only change us—convict us, give us wisdom for more and better action, sustain us in the overwhelming struggle—but would also change our leaders, those in power, and ultimately the world. As we pray and encounter God, we can't help but be spurred on to action. In other words, the more we pray about an issue, the more we realize what we can do. Prayer is empowering!

We read that in the midst of Nehemiah's moment of fear, he quickly prayed to God for wisdom. As the story goes, Nehemiah's words convinced the king to let him leave his position and lead a revival whose cornerstone was rebuilding Jerusalem's walls—an act of protection, defiance, and justice.

It would be a mistake to view this as Nehemiah's quick one and done prayer. When we read the beginning of the story, we see that Nehemiah spent the days before this encounter with the king fasting, confessing, praying, and humbling himself in the name of his people before God. It was this prolonged intimate time with God that allowed him to have such a bold and successful encounter with King Artaxerxes.

There is no doubt that when Nehemiah heard the sad news of his homeland and its dire state, his heart was burdened. In fact, we read that, immediately after he heard about Jerusalem, he sat down, weeping and mourning for days. But his first response was one of humility and honesty—he knew he was powerless to change the circumstances and needed to petition God for his divine intervention.

When it comes to the call to pursue justice, we can react similarly to Nehemiah. We hear news of modern slavery around the world, we see people wandering our streets owing in part to systems they can't overcome, we read about families stricken by poverty and unable to send their children to school or even feed them nutritious food, and we feel the need to get involved somehow. We try to figure out which organizations can be trusted and which ones need to be reformed. We realize it's a near impossible task, and can feel overwhelmed at our powerlessness.

Nehemiah models for us how we can begin to respond: through passionate prayer and inspired action. After Nehemiah began rebuilding the wall, he encountered great opposition from those directly opposed—and even threats of violence. But once again, Nehemiah called the people to God's mission of justice and right living; once again, he sought counsel from God in prayer and God sustained him in his struggle. Nehemiah knew that his work was not his own to accomplish but was God's design for his people—this gave him a sense of resting in God's power, not his own. Bringing justice to the world isn't going to be accomplished by us, but by God.

We imitate Christ when we seek justice for ourselves and our neighbors. He lends us his compassion and his dreams for restoration. It's his hope to see all of creation restored to wholeness, so we pray passionately for justice to be done—"Thy kingdom come, thy will be done on earth as it is in heaven"; we pray for God to change us, to make us sensitive to the cries of injustice, and for the wisdom and courage to act; and finally, we pray for God to sustain us in the struggle. The battle is his, so we rest in his power.

Read Nehemiah 1 Together
Nehemiah's Prayer

1 The words of Nehemiah son of Hakaliah: In the month of Kislev in the twentieth year, while I was in the citadel of Susa,

2 Hanani, one of my brothers, came from Judah with some other men, and I questioned them about the Jewish remnant that had survived the exile, and also about Jerusalem.

3 They said to me, "Those who survived the exile and are back in the province are in great trouble and disgrace. The wall of Jerusalem is broken down, and its gates have been burned with fire."

4 When I heard these things, I sat down and wept. For some days I mourned and fasted and prayed before the God of heaven.

5 Then I said: "Lord, the God of heaven, the great and awesome God, who keeps his covenant of love with those who love him and keep his commandments,

6 let your ear be attentive and your eyes open to hear the prayer your servant is praying before you day and night for your servants, the people of Israel.

I confess the sins we Israelites, including myself and my father's family, have committed against you.

7 We have acted very wickedly toward you. We have not obeyed the commands, decrees and laws you gave your servant Moses.

8 Remember the instruction you gave your servant Moses, saying, 'If you are unfaithful, I will scatter you among the nations,

9 but if you return to me and obey my commands, then even if your exiled people are at the farthest horizon, I will gather them from there and bring them to the place I have chosen as a dwelling for my Name.'

10 They are your servants and your people, whom you redeemed by your great strength and your mighty hand.

11 Lord, let your ear be attentive to the prayer of this your servant and to the prayer of your servants who delight in revering your name. Give your servant success today by granting him favor in the presence of this man." I was cupbearer to the king.

Read Nehemiah 5 Together
Nehemiah Helps the Poor

1 Now the men and their wives raised a great outcry against their fellow Jews.

2 Some were saying, "We and our sons and daughters are numerous; in order for us to eat and stay alive, we must get grain."

3 Others were saying, "We are mortgaging our fields, our vineyards and our homes to get grain during the famine."

4 Still others were saying, "We have had to borrow money to pay the king's tax on our fields and vineyards.

5 Although we are of the same flesh and blood as our fellow Jews and though our children are as good as theirs, yet we have to subject our sons and daughters to slavery. Some of our daughters have already been enslaved, but we are powerless, because our fields and our vineyards belong to others."

6 When I heard their outcry and these charges, I was very angry.

7 I pondered them in my mind and then accused the nobles and officials. I told them, "You are charging your own people interest!" So I called together a large meeting to deal with them

8 and said: "As far as possible, we have bought back our fellow Jews who were sold to the Gentiles. Now you are selling your own people, only for them to be sold back to us!" They kept quiet, because they could find nothing to say.

9 So I continued, "What you are doing is not right. Shouldn't you walk in the fear of our God to avoid the reproach of our Gentile enemies?

10 I and my brothers and my men are also lending the people money and grain. But let us stop charging interest!

11 Give back to them immediately their fields, vineyards, olive groves and houses, and also the interest you are charging them - one percent of the money, grain, new wine and olive oil."

12 "We will give it back," they said. "And we will not demand anything more from them. We will do as you say." Then I summoned the priests and made the nobles and officials take an oath to do what they had promised.

13 I also shook out the folds of my robe and said, "In this way may God shake out of their house and possessions anyone who does not keep this promise. So may such a person be shaken out and emptied!" At this the whole assembly said, "Amen," and praised the Lord. And the people did as they had promised.

14 Moreover, from the twentieth year of King Artaxerxes, when I was appointed to be their governor in the land of Judah, until his thirty-second year - twelve years - neither I nor my brothers ate the food allotted to the governor.

15 But the earlier governors - those preceding me - placed a heavy burden on the people and took forty shekels of silver from them in addition to food and wine. Their assistants also lorded it over the people. But out of reverence for God I did not act like that.

16 Instead, I devoted myself to the work on this wall. All my men were assembled there for the work; we did not acquire any land.

17 Furthermore, a hundred and fifty Jews and officials ate at my table, as well as those who came to us from the surrounding nations.

18 Each day one ox, six choice sheep and some poultry were prepared for me, and every ten days an abundant supply of wine of all kinds. In spite of all this, I never demanded the food allotted to the governor, because the demands were heavy on these people.

19 Remember me with favor, my God, for all I have done for these people.

Questions for Discussion

1. Are there things you pray for daily?

   _____

   _____

   _____

2. Do you pray about "big" issues like hunger, slavery, extreme poverty? What do those prayers look like?

   _____

   _____

   _____

3. How does Nehemiah's prayer life empower him to have confidence in pursuing justice for God's people? How can we pray in the same way for our context?

   _____

   _____

   _____

4. Share a time when your prayers were clearly answered.

   _____

   _____

   _____

5. What is God saying to you, and what are you going to do about it?

   _____

   _____

   _____

Together

Print off, cut out from newspapers, or draw pictures that represent strength, power and wealth: pictures of politicians, corporate logos, etc. Then do the same with pictures that represent the most vulnerable people and places in our world: children, widows, a map of an impoverished community, etc. As a group, look at these pictures side by side. Pray that the vulnerable might influence the powerful and that the powerful will use their strength to seek justice for the vulnerable. Pray specifically for your leaders and the decisions they make that impact poor and vulnerable people in your country and around the world.

Solo Work

Begin writing your long-term action plan.[2] From this session onwards you will continue to add to your personal action plan. All of your action commitments should be measurable and time-bound. You'll eventually share this action plan with your group to help remind you of your commitments. Begin with a prayer commitment. Challenge yourself to pray about an issue that seems too big or too overwhelming, and pray daily for a month. This will train you to come to God persistently and prayerfully in the face of injustice. Additionally, consider one way in which you will mobilize your community to be in prayer. Keep working on your creative expression.

Prayer

Lord, give me the dedication of Nehemiah to see justice done even in the face of adversity. Draw me close to you, and your concerns. Give me sensitive ears and eyes, to hear and see injustice, and the courage to respond.

2 See page 82 for a template you can use to begin filling out your long term action plan

Justice and Advocacy: Using your voice to campaign for justice

"If you are neutral in situations of injustice you have chosen the side of the oppressor."
Desmond Tutu

"It is impossible to ignore the political implications of biblical justice." Joel Edwards

Definitions

G8 (or Group of 8): A forum for the governments of eight of the leading economies in the world, who periodically came together to discuss issues of global concern. The member states included Canada, France, Germany, Italy, Japan, Russia, the United Kingdom, and the United States of America.

Advocacy: Challenging ourselves or our leaders to change attitudes, behaviors or policies that perpetuate injustice.

Advocacy saves lives

Elinata Kasanga lives in Nguluka Village, Zambia. Elinata remembers a time in her village's history when there was a lack of basic necessities. People couldn't afford health clinic fees or school fees. Most villagers survived on one meal a day and on water from contaminated local streams. The lack of basic necessities was made worse by the fact that the government of Zambia owed billions of dollars to governments of wealthier countries. Money spent servicing debt payments, but failing to keep pace as the interest grew, was money not going to help the impoverished.

People around the world began to take action, with Christians at the forefront, believing it was unreasonable to enforce debt payments at the expense of basic necessities of life. Thus, the Jubilee 2000 campaign began, advocating for the cancellation of debts that impoverished nations could not afford to pay to richer countries in the Global North and to the World Bank, as a way to celebrate the millennium in the year 2000. The year of Jubilee (Leviticus 25) was built upon the assumption that left unchecked, the social, political, and economic order would tear communities apart because of greed and unjust practices. Jubilee was a chance to hit reset, and Jubilee 2000 was a chance to apply that biblical principle in modern times.

More than 24 million people signed the Jubilee 2000 petition. Signatures, including thumbprints and email petitions, were collected from more than 155 countries. The petition was delivered to the United Nations Millennium Summit in September 2000. There were national organizations and campaigns in more than sixty countries, which lobbied, campaigned, protested, and educated. Activities varied from grassroots letter-writing campaigns targeting MPs, to national rallies with high-level celebrities, united by the symbol of human chains.

Jubilee 2000 succeeded in getting large amounts of debt canceled for qualifying countries, but it didn't stop there. People around the world have continued to campaign, and since 1996, over $130 billion of poor countries' debts have been canceled.

Because of this, the public health centers in Elinata's community are now fully stocked with medicine and schools are free for grades 1 to 7. For the first time, Elinata and her community have access to clean water.

Beyond Nguluka Village, after debts were canceled:

- 1.5 million children returned to school in Uganda after the government eliminated school fees;

- 500,000 children in Mozambique received vaccinations;

- Free health care was provided for millions living in rural areas in Zambia, many of whom had never had access to any form of modern health care before;

- 2,500 new primary schools were created and 28,000 extra teachers were trained, resulting in 98 percent of Tanzanian children being able to enroll in primary education.

Desmond Tutu once said, "There comes a point where we need to stop just pulling people out of the river. We need to go upstream and find out why they're falling in." Jubilee did just that and continues to transform lives to date. Many people were changed by taking part in the campaign, seeing that a huge injustice can be a normal part of how the world works, and finding their voice to help overcome it.

Social Sin,
by Ronald J. Sider

It is possible to make oppression legal. Legislators devise unjust laws, and bureaucrats implement the injustice. But God shouts a divine woe against rulers who use their official position to write unjust laws and unfair legal decisions. Legalized oppression is an abomination to our God. Therefore, God calls his people to oppose political structures that perpetuate injustice.

There is a long tradition of God's people challenging the political structures of the day, beginning with Moses going to Pharaoh, Esther to the Persian King, William Wilberforce to end the transatlantic slave trade, Dr. King and the US civil rights movement, all the way up to Christians of today speaking out against corruption and policies that perpetuate injustice.

However, neglect of the biblical teaching on structural injustice or institutionalized evil is one of the most deadly omissions in many parts of the church today. Christians frequently restrict ethics to a narrow class of "personal" sins such as drug abuse and sexual misconduct but ignore the sins of institutionalized racism and unjust economic structures that destroy just as many people.

There is an important difference between consciously willed, individual acts (like lying to a friend or committing an act of adultery) and participation in evil social structures. Slavery is an example of the latter. So is the Victorian factory system that had ten-year-old children working twelve to sixteen hours a day. Both slavery and child labor were legal, but they destroyed millions of people. They were institutionalized, or structural, evils.

God hates evil economic structures and unjust legal systems because they destroy people by the hundreds and thousands and millions. We can be sure that the just Lord of the universe will destroy wicked rulers and unjust social institutions (see 1 Kings 21).

Another side to institutionalized evil makes it especially pernicious. Structural evil is so subtle that we become ensnared without fully realizing it. God inspired the prophet Amos to utter some of the harshest words in scripture against the cultured upper-class women of his day: "hear this word you cows of Bashan...who oppress the poor, who crush the needy, who say to your husbands, 'bring, that we may drink!' The Lord God has sworn by his holiness that, behold the days are coming when they shall take you away with hooks, even the last of you with fishhooks" (4:1-2).

The women involved may have had a little direct contact with the impoverished peasants. They may never have fully realized that their gorgeous cloth and spirited parties were possible partly because of the sweat and tears of the poor. In fact, they may have even been kind on occasion to individuals in oppression. But God called these privileged women "cows" because they participated in a structural evil—lives sustained by the oppression of others. Before God, they were personally and individually guilty.

If we are members of a privileged group that profits from structural evil, or whose lives are sustained by the oppression of others, and if we have at least some understanding of the evil yet fail to do what God wants us to do to change things, we stand guilty before God.

Unfair systems and oppressive structures are an abomination to God, and "social sin" is the correct phrase to categorize them. Furthermore, as we understand their evil, we have a moral obligation to do all God wants us to do to change them. If we do not, we sin. That is the clear implication of Amos' harsh attack on the wealthy women of his day. It is also the clear implication of James 4:17, "Whoever knows what is right to do and fails to do it, for him it is sin."

In the New Testament, the Word cosmos (world) often conveys the idea of structural evil. In Greek thought, the word cosmos referred to the structures of civilized life, especially the patterns of the Greek city-state that were viewed as essentially good. But the biblical writers knew that sin had invaded and distorted the structures and values of society.

Frequently, therefore, the New Testament uses the word cosmos to refer, in C. H. Dodd's words, "to human society in so far as it is organized on wrong principles". "When Paul spoke of 'the world' in a moral sense, he was thinking of the totality of people, social systems, values, and traditions in terms of its opposition to God and his redemptive purposes".

Pope John Paul II has rightly insisted that evil social structures are "rooted in personal sin". Social evil results from our rebellion against God and our consequent selfishness toward our neighbors. But the accumulation and concentration of many personal sins create "structures of sin" that are both oppressive and difficult to remove. We will not see transformed systems simply by converting every CEO, employee of multinational corporations, and member of Congress. We will see transformation by preaching the gospel while dismantling unjust structures and systems through effective advocacy, passionate prayer and living justly.

Read Esther 3:1-11, 4:13-14 and 8:3-8 Together

1 After these events, King Xerxes honored Haman son of Hammedatha, the Agagite, elevating him and giving him a seat of honor higher than that of all the other nobles.

2 All the royal officials at the king's gate knelt down and paid honor to Haman, for the king had commanded this concerning him. But Mordecai would not kneel down or pay him honor.

3 Then the royal officials at the king's gate asked Mordecai, "Why do you disobey the king's command?"

4 Day after day they spoke to him but he refused to comply. Therefore they told Haman about it to see whether Mordecai's behavior would be tolerated, for he had told them he was a Jew.

5 When Haman saw that Mordecai would not kneel down or pay him honor, he was enraged.

6 Yet having learned who Mordecai's people were, he scorned the idea of killing only Mordecai. Instead Haman looked for a way to destroy all Mordecai's people, the Jews, throughout the whole kingdom of Xerxes.

7 In the twelfth year of King Xerxes, in the first month, the month of Nisan, the pur (that is, the lot) was cast in the presence of Haman to select a day and month. And the lot fell on the twelfth month, the month of Adar.

8 Then Haman said to King Xerxes, "There is a certain people dispersed among the peoples in all the provinces of your kingdom who keep themselves separate. Their customs are different from those of all other people, and they do not obey the king's laws; it is not in the king's best interest to tolerate them.

9 If it pleases the king, let a decree be issued to destroy them, and I will give ten thousand talents of silver to the king's administrators for the royal treasury."

10 So the king took his signet ring from his finger and gave it to Haman son of Hammedatha, the Agagite, the enemy of the Jews.

11 "Keep the money," the king said to Haman, "and do with the people as you please."

Esther 4:13-14

13 "Do not think that because you are in the king's house you alone of all the Jews will escape.

14 For if you remain silent at this time, relief and deliverance for the Jews will arise from another place, but you and your father's family will perish. And who knows but that you have come to your royal position for such a time as this?"

Esther 8:3-8

3 Esther again pleaded with the king, falling at his feet and weeping. She begged him to put an end to the evil plan of Haman the Agagite, which he had devised against the Jews.

4 Then the king extended the gold scepter to Esther and she arose and stood before him.

5 "If it pleases the king," she said, "and if he regards me with favor and thinks it the right thing to do, and if he is pleased with me, let an order be written overruling the dispatches that Haman son of Hammedatha, the Agagite, devised and wrote to destroy the Jews in all the king's provinces.

6 For how can I bear to see disaster fall on my people? How can I bear to see the destruction of my family?"

7 King Xerxes replied to Queen Esther and to Mordecai the Jew, "Because Haman attacked the Jews, I have given his estate to Esther, and they have impaled him on the pole he set up.

8 Now write another decree in the king's name on behalf of the Jews as seems best to you, and seal it with the king's signet ring – for no document written in the king's name and sealed with his ring can be revoked."

Questions for Discussion

1. Why is Esther hesitant to speak to the king at first?

2. What is the value of Mordecai influencing Esther to advocate for her people, and what are the implications for our understanding of political advocacy today?

3. Both Esther's advocacy and the Jubilee 2000 movement were inspired by the call of those in oppression for advocacy to challenge injustice. Can you think of examples of this in modern advocacy movements?

4. What are the risks if those who are experiencing injustice have no voice in our advocacy?

5. What is God saying to you, and what are you going to do about it?

Together

Demystify advocacy by pulling out a cell phone and calling your member of Congress on the spot. They're probably not in the office, but that's okay. Put it on speakerphone and have one person leave a message. Whether someone answers the phone or you leave a message, begin by letting your member of Congress know that you are participating in a small group study on justice and presently addressing the importance of advocacy.[3]

Describe how you're learning about the incredible impact (for such a low cost!) of poverty-focused development assistance, and urge your representative to be a champion for the impoverished by protecting this funding in budget negotiations. If you leave a message, invite the representative to respond by calling back a designated member of your group.

Solo Work

Think of one way you can promote justice or speak out and be a voice for justice to your leaders. Commit to something specific—maybe it's a promise to organize an advocacy training for your church or a commitment to write one letter a month to your government on a justice-related issue. Add this commitment to your action plan.

Prayer

Lord, give me the courage to take risks the way Esther did, and to challenge injustice, even if it is at great cost to me. Help me to steward my voice and advocate for justice with my elected officials. Be with our government and leaders who make major decisions that impact people all over the world. Give them wisdom, tenderness, and sensitivity to the cries of those living in poverty.

3 Call script, background information, detailed instructions on how to call congress and more on page 84

Justice and Consumption: Possessions are not power

"The witness to simplicity is profoundly rooted in the biblical tradition, and most perfectly exemplified in the life of Jesus Christ."
Richard J. Foster

"When we recognize that the people who make our stuff have hopes, dreams, and personalities, we can't help but care about whether their job pays them a living wage and allows them to reach those dreams." Kelsey Timmerman

Definitions

Fairtrade: A system of selling and buying goods that ensures greater justice and fairness in trade. Farmers and workers get better prices and wages, decent working conditions, and fairer terms of trade.

Cooperative: A farm, business, or other organization that is owned and run jointly by its members, who share the profits or benefits. Cooperatives are based on the values of self-help, self-responsibility, democracy, equality, equity, and solidarity.

Simplicity: Cultivating a lifestyle of modesty in consumption. When we choose to live simply, we consume less, which in turn aids in the decreased demand for goods produced cheaply and often unjustly.

The Value of Cotton

Makandianfing Keita[4] is a cotton farmer from Mali. Before joining a cooperative, his family struggled to survive because cotton prices were going down and down until they were below the cost of production. Because of this, the community struggled:

- Children had to walk 10km to go to school, which made school unattainable for many,

- Pregnant women had no access to health care. Many died in childbirth and there were high rates of infant mortality,

- The environment was often degraded through the use of dangerous pesticides, burning, and soil erosion.

In 2005, the village farmers joined a cotton cooperative. This means that their cotton would now be bought at fair trade prices that were significantly higher than the artificially low market

---

4 This story is based on an interview by Rachel Dixon and used by permission. Copyright Guardian News & Media Ltd, 2016

rates, and that the farmers would together decide how to invest their income. After joining the cooperative, they were able to make immense progress. Within the first three years:

- They built a school in the community. At first, it had two classrooms. When they had more money and wanted to expand, they challenged the government to match their investment. Now there are five classrooms in total, and every child in the village can go to school.

- They built a maternity center.

- They installed a pump for drinking water.

- They built a new road, enabling farmers to travel further than 5km outside of the village with ease.

The commitment and demand of consumers to buy cotton at a fairly traded price, coupled with Makandianfing and his community's commitment to justice and flourishing in their community, made these developments possible.

The cost of cotton was literally killing Makandianfing's community, but following the changes implemented by him, his community, and consumers, the value of cotton helped his community flourish.

Every time we consume goods we can perpetuate either the suffering or the flourishing of others.

Possessions Are Not Power,
by José Marcos da Silva

We live in a world where our attitudes and actions are strongly influenced by cultural models—often, without us realizing it. One such cultural model is consumerism, which carries with it the illusion that "possessions are power." We are led to believe that people are only the sum of what they possess. Clothes, accessories, buildings, cars, electronics, restaurants, hotels: these define who we are. Our buying power and consumption define our identity.

We are encouraged to have as many things as possible, to consume as much as we can, and to throw away anything we no longer want. As a result, our lifestyles are now largely unsustainable and require urgent and radical change. With this in mind, let's pause to ask ourselves: What guidance can the Bible give us on how to approach consumption? What is the relationship between what we own and consume, and our Christian beliefs?

At the beginning of the Bible, in Genesis, God gave us a mandate to steward the earth. However, people often want the maximum results from the minimum effort, and this leads to exploitation. This has been particularly obvious in our relationship with God's creation. We were not made to exploit God's creation until it no longer exists; we were called to work it and take care of it (Genesis 2:15). We have a spiritual responsibility for God's creation. Instead of squandering its resources, we must use them carefully and sustainably. This begs some key questions: What can we do to reduce our consumption? Do we really need everything we possess? How can we consume in a way that's more ethical and sustainable?

Another theological concept that must inform our consumption is abundant life or full life. The Greek word that some versions of the Bible translate as "abundant" (an abundant life) is also translated as "full" (a full life). There is a big difference between abundance and fullness: abundance implies more than is necessary, and fullness suggests harmony. Our lives can only be full when they are in harmony, and this also includes our relationship with what we own and consume.

The ideology that promotes the concept of "the more we own, the more blessed we are by God" has grown in recent times, leading vast numbers of believers to want more and more. This idea is more closely linked to that of abundance, but actually, the life that Christ means us to have is a "full life," where we have just enough in order to live in peace (shalom) with God. How does this work in practice? We may not have an expensive mattress, but we are still able to sleep soundly; we may not live in a mansion, but we still have safe shelter. Jesus reminds us that we should look to the birds of the air and the lilies of the field (Matthew 6:26-34), so we can comprehend God's love and desire to bless us. However, without us sharing what we have, there are many who aren't seeing their material needs met, and it is our privilege to work as a channel of blessing to others.

Jesus' teaching on God vs. Mammon (Matthew 6:24) would be a direct challenge to the consumerism of today. Mammon is the Gentile God of riches attained through greed and covetousness. For the love of money, many wander from the faith (1 Timothy 6:10). Throughout the Bible as a whole, there is a tension between the love of money and the love of God. We cannot love both, as they both compete to reign over us, and no man can serve two masters without displeasing one. Accumulating possessions is widely accepted in capitalist culture. It is now so extreme that one percent of the richest people in the world own the same amount as the rest of the population. This is completely unjust! Despite this, it is still considered normal to want as much as possible for ourselves. We focus most of our attention and energy on accumulating and earning more, without realizing that this path takes us further from God's plan, and that the false abundance will only lead to misery.

Another impact of the unrestrained quest for profit at any cost can be seen in the exploitation of workers, driven by the demand from consumers. In much of the business world where the priority is to make an ever-greater profit, there is a toxic tendency to ignore ethical and human principles. The exploitation of labor is a form of slavery. This means that not only is it important for us to consume only what is necessary but that it is also important for us to think about the origins of what we buy.

What are the practical implications of these scriptural values for us here today?

If we want to be disciples of Christ, we must try to imitate him. Jesus was a humble servant. He was holy and lived a radically simple life. These three characteristics are profoundly entwined, and they should underlie our discipleship.

Someone once said that "wisdom is learning to love people and use things." The opposite is destructive. If we love things and use people, we cause pain and destruction. The things we have should be at the service of our neighbors, and never the contrary.

Our priority should not be to accumulate things, as this can destroy both us and God's creation. Possessions are not power. Giving is power! Generosity is essential. This Christian model is one that in many places the world has forgotten, and if we can embrace it in our own attitudes, we will honor Christ.

If we can consider the relationship between buying and consuming in the light of these values, everything else will follow naturally. We will take care of nature because that is our role, and its restoration is part of the plan of salvation (Romans 8:19-25); we will consume fewer things more responsibly; and we will not rush off in search of wealth, because the love of riches distances us from God. We will lead simple lives, as we seek to follow and imitate Jesus.

Read Jeremiah 22:13-17 Together

13 "Woe to him who builds his palace by unrighteousness, his upper rooms by injustice, making his own people work for nothing, not paying them for their labor.

14 He says, 'I will build myself a great palace with spacious upper rooms.' So he makes large windows in it, panels it with cedar and decorates it in red.

15 Does it make you a king to have more and more cedar? Did not your father have food and drink? He did what was right and just, so all went well with him.

16 He defended the cause of the poor and needy, and so all went well. Is that not what it means to know me?" declares the Lord.

17 "But your eyes and your heart are set only on dishonest gain, on shedding innocent blood and on oppression and extortion."

Questions for Discussion

1. What specific acts or situations of injustice are found in this passage?

    _____

    _____

    _____

2. Contrast the two kinds mentioned in the Jeremiah passage. What was the problem with the son's wealth?

    _____

    _____

    _____

3. Do you know who/what sustains your lifestyle? Share with the group about one way you try to seek justice with your consumption.

    _____

    _____

    _____

4. What is God saying to you, and what are you going to do about it?

    _____

    _____

    _____

Together

One way we can ensure our consumption is not contributing to the suffering of others is by reducing the amount of goods we buy, reusing those goods we can through repair, and repurposing and recycling goods that we cannot reuse. By doing so we reduce waste, lower the demand for cheap, unjustly produced goods, and also resist the prevailing culture that puts too much value on material things as a source of satisfaction. Some of us live this way by choice, and others of us do this out of economic necessity. Now is your chance to share with your group your clever ideas! What is one way you and your family have reused or recycled items and, in turn, reduced consumption?

Solo Work

Research one product that you often buy. Find out how the company that produces it treats its employees. Try to research the supply chain: how are those who made or grew the product treated?

- Does this influence your desire to continue buying goods from this company? How can you buy from more justice-oriented companies? Come prepared to share your findings with the group.

- Add a "consumption" piece to your action plan. Make it specific. How can you live more simply? How can you buy more ethically? Maybe commit to buy from a local company that you know treats its employees well. Maybe commit to only buy fair trade coffee or used clothing. Pick one thing you can make actionable and embrace it for the long haul!

- Continue to work on your creative expression and find one person to share your thoughts, ideas, and even your project with, to get feedback and to help you in your creative process.

Prayer

Lord, forgive me for the times I consume goods selfishly or unwisely, without regard for my impact on others. Help me to be aware of how I consume on a daily basis and how I can promote the flourishing of others through my choices. Help me to live justly in the area of consumption. Not as someone seeking to keep the "justice" laws, but rather as an act of worship towards you.

Justice and Generosity: Justice will cost you something

"If our giving does not at all pinch or hamper us, I should say it is too small. There ought to be things we should like to do and cannot because our commitment to giving excludes them." C.S. Lewis

"It's not how much we give but how much love we put into giving." Mother Teresa

Definitions

Sacrificial Giving: Giving from our substance rather than abundance.

Sacrificial Giving

I remember hearing a story about my grandfather that caused me to rethink what it means to be generous. Many of us struggle to give ten percent of our earnings away; how much harder would it be to do if that ten percent meant one less meal for you or your family?

On his way home from work he encountered a man on the street who was clearly in need, and this man shared his story—he was visiting their town for the very first time, he had come here for work, had been robbed, his car had broken down, and the job turned out to be a scam. Basically, everything that could go wrong on this first visit went wrong. Even though my grandfather did not have abundance, he brought the man home for dinner with his family, prayed for him, and gave him some money before the man left. His family didn't think too much of this stranger at dinner as it was their practice to all eat a little less in order to make a plate for my grandfather's frequent unexpected guests.

A few years later, my grandfather returned home from work with a stranger in tow for dinner. However, he actually wasn't a stranger. It was the same man from a few years ago—the one with the very unique and unforgettable story. And somehow, the exact same fate that had befallen him years before had occurred once again; however, he did not recall my grandfather or his family. After a déjà vu dinner, my grandfather once again prayed for the man and gave him some money before the man went on his way. My grandfather's family asked whether he remembered that this man had told them the same story a few years before, and it was clearly a lie. My grandfather replied, "Of course I knew it was the same man, and that his story was not true, but imagine how much need he must be to lie in order to survive?" I always think of this story whenever I am tempted to hoard what God has given me. My grandfather gave at a cost to himself and his family, but rooted in his trust of God, he gave sacrificially.

Combating Greed with Generosity, *by Gaston Slanwa*

In such an unequal world, the need for justice and generosity is greater than ever before. Generosity is also a clear biblical command.

A dictionary may define generosity as the quality of being kind and generous, but it is important to also understand that biblical generosity is the result of a transformed heart. We give because God loved us first and because we long to love, live and give as he did. We want to grab hold of "life in all its fullness" (John 10:10), of which giving is an important part. We are told by Jesus himself that "it is more blessed to give than to receive" (Acts 20:35). By giving, we are also able to help release the hold that money can create on our hearts. "Command those who are rich in this present world … to do good, to be rich in good deeds, and to be generous and willing to share … so that they may take hold of the life that is truly life" (1 Timothy 6:17-19). Scripture teaches that our heart can't serve two masters, and by being generous with what God has given us we're able to release its hold on our lives and put our trust in him. **Every time we give generously, and even sacrificially, we are putting our trust in God rather than in our wealth.**

Today our world is extremely polarized by wealth and poverty. The rich/poor divide is not just one between nations but also within every nation and every community. Poverty from a biblical perspective is broken relationships: with God, with ourselves, with others, with our communities, and with our environment. In seeking to be part of God's kingdom working to restore these relationships, one of our challenges is to give generously to meet the needs of the most vulnerable.

While wealth is sometimes considered a blessing, there is also a clear responsibility to share wealth with others, and in the Old Testament there is even an implication that extreme wealth often comes through exploitation.

We must also consider the plight of the poor in a world of excess. In the United States, the richest fifty people have as much wealth as the poorest 165 million. Think about that—165 million people have as much as fifty people.

While clearly Jesus was preaching the good news to all, he showed throughout his ministry the particular interest in the poor and the downtrodden that God has always had. Jesus, in his incarnation, "moved in" with the poor. He lived with, ate with, and associated with the socially ostracized (Matt 9:13).

And now, unlike any time in history, those who seek to follow Jesus need to be aware of the magnitude of the suffering and injustice in the world and to be real and effective instruments of justice in an unjust world.

Scripture shows that God hears the cries of those who are poor; delivers justice on their behalf; defends and protects them; is angry with those who abuse and oppress them; and identifies with them. God sets himself against those who practice injustice and are not generous toward those in need.

We have a clear call to give generously, following the pattern of our Master and Lord Jesus Christ, who gave everything in order that we can be saved and blessed. The opposite of the love of money is generosity. Instead of looking to take, we are invited to give, for there is always more joy in giving than receiving.

The need for justice and generosity in our world is immense. Justice and generosity will surely bring healing to our world. God is a just and generous God. Those who profess to be his children must seek to resemble him.

Read Isaiah 58:4-10 Together

4 Your fasting ends in quarreling and strife, and in striking each other with wicked fists. You cannot fast as you do today and expect your voice to be heard on high.

5 Is this the kind of fast I have chosen, only a day for people to humble themselves? Is it only for bowing one's head like a reed and for lying in sackcloth and ashes? Is that what you call a fast, a day acceptable to the Lord?

6 Is not this the kind of fasting I have chosen: to loose the chains of injustice and untie the cords of the yoke, to set the oppressed free and break every yoke?

7 Is it not to share your food with the hungry and to provide the poor wanderer with shelter— when you see the naked, to clothe them, and not to turn away from your own flesh and blood?

8 Then your light will break forth like the dawn, and your healing will quickly appear; then your righteousness will go before you, and the glory of the Lord will be your rear guard.

9 Then you will call, and the Lord will answer; you will cry for help, and he will say: Here am I. If you do away with the yoke of oppression, with the pointing finger and malicious talk,

10 and if you spend yourselves in behalf of the hungry and satisfy the needs of the oppressed, then your light will rise in the darkness, and your night will become like the noonday.

Questions for Discussion

1. It is clear in Isaiah 58 that God wants us to "spend" ourselves; this means giving of ourselves. How do you define giving sacrificially?

   _____

   _____

   _____

2. What does the passage describe as the benefits of living generously?

   _____

   _____

   _____

3. Fasting is often considered a form of worship that shows great devotion. What does Isaiah 58 teach us about acts of justice as worship?

   _____

   _____

   _____

4. What is God saying to you, and what are you going to do about it?

   _____

   _____

   _____

Together

Today, you will all leave with one less thing than you came with. Empty your pockets. Yep, right now. Practicing generosity when we least expect it is a good reminder of our posture toward our possessions. Everything we have is God's; as a reminder of that today, offer up the cash in your pocket, the shoes on your feet, or the watch on your wrist. Put these in a pile in the middle of the room and snap a photo. Make sure everyone gets a copy of the photo—and keep it as a reminder of sacrificial living.

Collectively decide where to donate these things, but more significantly, pray that this will be more than an exercise—the beginning of great sacrifice in your lives for justice. The photo will always be a reminder of the radical generosity that God calls us to.

Solo Work

Examine your heart. What is holding you back from giving generously and sacrificially? Take a moment to pray and listen. It could be a trust issue, it could be a sense of ownership over your money and time, it could be a selfish desire to have more, and so on.

_____

_____

_____

Write down the barriers you have to giving. How can you sacrificially give of yourself moving forward? Think of one to three ideas for your action plan related to giving more of yourself—your money, your time, and/or your energy.

_____

_____

_____

Continue to work on your creative expression.

Prayer

Lord, help me to be generous, to give freely of what I have, because everything I have has been given to me by you. Help me to put my trust in you.

Justice and Relationships: Solidarity is the heart of relationship

"When people begin moving beyond charity and toward justice and solidarity with the poor and oppressed, as Jesus did, they get in trouble. Once we are actually friends with the folks in struggle, we start to ask why people are poor, which is never as popular as giving to charity." Shane Claiborne

"You can't lead the people if you don't love the people. You can't save the people if you don't serve the people." Dr. Cornel Wes

The Solidarity of Christ

Solidarity as a Christian practice is not something we teach in Sunday school, but we ought to. We often use this word in association with other things like generosity, empathy, or support. But it means far more than any one of these single ideas.

The most compelling example of solidarity in all of history is Christ himself.

God becoming human, becoming one of us—not just suffering like us, but suffering with us—is the greatest act of solidarity. God knows what we go through because he became one of us. There is no solidarity greater than this. Solidarity is the foundation of relationship.

Jesus not only demonstrates solidarity but demands it of us, his followers.

The fundamental revelation in Jesus' teaching, often called "The Sheep and Goats" (Matthew 25), is that Jesus himself experiences a cosmic-level solidarity with the suffering, and that what we do to the "least of these brothers and sisters" we do unto him. He did not use this parable inspirationally, as in "Imagine that the hungry, the thirsty, the stranger, the naked, the sick and the imprisoned are me, and treat them the way you would treat me, someone you love and serve." Instead, he spoke in a declarative way that violates our understanding of time and space: "What you have done to the least of these you have done unto me."

It is cosmic. It is final. Jesus is in such deep solidarity with the suffering that he experiences what they experience. He experiences their suffering, rejection, hunger, and thirst, but he also experiences their relief! Can you imagine giving Jesus a meal? It is beyond our comprehension yet demands action from us.

One of my favorite meditations on the solidarity of Christ comes from John Mark McMillan's song, "The Road, the Rocks, and the Weeds":

Come down from your mountain, your high-rise apartment

And tell me of the God you know who bleeds

And what to tell my daughter when she asks so many questions

And I fail to fill her heaviness with peace

When I've got no answers for hurt knees or cancers

But a Savior who suffers them with me

Singing goodbye, Olympus, the heart of my Maker

Is spread out on the road, the rocks, and the weeds

Relationship: the foundation of justice, *by Sunia Gibbs*

Where I live and work, I can't walk very far without seeing or passing someone who is houseless. When I first moved into the city, there were mornings I would walk out my front door and I would find one or two individuals taking shelter on the porch to avoid the rain or sleeping off a hard night. In the beginning, I wanted to give and share with every single person. I handed out sleeping pads and blankets, shared food, prayed, and offered advice. But the longer I lived in the city, the more I

gave, and the more frequently I heard a knock on my door, the more I became tired and numb. The need was never-ending but my compassion was not. I felt used. I worried about how much I could give without compromising my children or our home, and I didn't really know whether anything I was doing even mattered. I was disillusioned and disappointed.

To endure in the work of justice we must determinedly walk through the wastelands produced by greed, lust, and loss and not run away when overwhelmed with disparity. The anecdote for quitting or disillusionment is not simply greater zeal, but increased love and compassion that comes from the Spirit of God living in each of us.

Every relationship—from our immediate family to the stranger we care for—ought to be founded, directed, and empowered by love. In 1 Corinthians 13:3, Paul tells us that if we give everything to the poor, or even become martyrs, but do not have love, there is no benefit.

This is an important reminder for those who dedicate their lives to the work of justice. The just life we are called to live cannot ignore the needs of our spouses or children or closest friends. At the same time, the just life we are called to live cannot ignore the needs of our brothers and sisters on the street or around the world because their burden is ours. Jesus demonstrated the solidarity we ought to have in Matthew 25:40 when he said, "Whatever was done to the least of these who are members of my family, you did it to me." These words brought encouragement to the disciples who were being sent into the world. They would remember that whatever was being done to them was felt and known by Jesus, their brother, Savior and friend. As the body of Christ, are we aware of the pain in other parts of the body? How can we act/speak in solidarity with one another just like Christ does for each of us?

Love for God and love for neighbor empower and eradicate the distance between every human being. When we begin to truly comprehend that the Word became flesh and walked with us (John 1:14), we will have a deeper understanding of humility and self-sacrificing love. Think of it: the one who is divine and holy put on frail humanity and made his home with us. Emmanuel—God with us.

Who are we with? If we ignore or avoid the vulnerable around us, how can we be motivated to act with them for deliverance? If our eyes only see people exactly like us, if we just work really hard in order to purchase shiny new objects, or if all our energy is spent striving for higher positions of power or fame, we have given in to the values of the world around us instead of becoming increasingly responsive to the Spirit of God, who reminds us of our abundance and compels us to go deeper and generously into our communities.

Jesus lived with the poor. He saw them and was moved with compassion and met their needs. Are we empowered and free to do the same? 1 John 3:16-18 encourages us in this way: "This is how we know what love is: Jesus Christ laid down his life for us. And we ought to lay down our lives for our brothers and sisters. If anyone has material possessions and sees a brother or sister in need but has no pity on them, how can the love of God be in that person? Dear children, let us not love with words or speech but with actions and in truth."

We demonstrate love through our relationships with one another. And this love must be more than the words we speak, but also the actions we take to relieve one another's burdens. It is the only way our love can be sincere. It is the way in which we prove we know God's love. It's not in how many verses we've memorized or in keeping our religious rituals, but in how we love one another.

May our relationships with one another radiate and demonstrate the abundant and generous love of God. May we have the courage and empowerment to live justly with and towards one another.

Read Matthew 25:31–46 Together

The Sheep and the Goats

31 "When the Son of Man comes in his glory, and all the angels with him, he will sit on his glorious throne.

32 All the nations will be gathered before him, and he will separate the people one from another as a shepherd separates the sheep from the goats.

33 He will put the sheep on his right and the goats on his left.

34 Then the King will say to those on his right, 'Come, you who are blessed by my Father; take your inheritance, the kingdom prepared for you since the creation of the world.

35 For I was hungry and you gave me something to eat, I was thirsty and you gave me something to drink, I was a stranger and you invited me in,

36 I needed clothes and you clothed me, I was sick and you looked after me, I was in prison and you came to visit me.'

37 Then the righteous will answer him, 'Lord, when did we see you hungry and feed you, or thirsty and give you something to drink?

38 When did we see you a stranger and invite you in, or needing clothes and clothe you?

39 When did we see you sick or in prison and go to visit you?'

40 The King will reply, 'Truly I tell you, whatever you did for one of the least of these brothers and sisters of mine, you did for me.'

41 Then he will say to those on his left, 'Depart from me, you who are cursed, into the eternal fire prepared for the devil and his angels.

42 For I was hungry and you gave me nothing to eat, I was thirsty and you gave me nothing to drink,

43 I was a stranger and you did not invite me in, I needed clothes and you did not clothe me, I was sick and in prison and you did not look after me.'

44 They also will answer, 'Lord, when did we see you hungry or thirsty or a stranger or needing clothes or sick or in prison, and did not help you?'

45 He will reply, 'Truly I tell you, whatever you did not do for one of the least of these, you did not do for me.'

46 Then they will go away to eternal punishment, but the righteous to eternal life."

Questions for Discussion

1. How does Jesus challenge us in our relationships?

_____

_____

_____

2. Who are the "least of these" in our world?

_____

_____

_____

3. How has this session challenged your ideas about solidarity, and what it means for us?

_____

_____

_____

4. What is God saying to you, and what are you going to do about it?

_____

_____

_____

Together

Humility and vulnerability should be at the core of all of our relationships. In the context of seeking justice, this is true both with the impoverished and with our loved ones. This next exercise is a practice in both!

Have someone in the group read John 13:1-17. During the reading, begin taking off your shoes and socks. Once you are all barefoot, have the person read it again. Let the reality of this incredible act of humility, the Son of God washing the feet of his disciples, sink in.

Start praying together as a group for you to form authentic relationships with one another, for opportunities to be in relationship with people in oppression, and for strong relationships with your loved ones. Pray as the Holy Spirit leads you.

As you are praying, have one person begin by washing the feet of the person on his or her left. Afterwards, that person washes the feet of the next person to the left, and so on until all of you (who wish to) have participated.

Solo Work

Reflect on your own relationships. Make a list of the ten people you engage with most regularly. What does the list tell you? Are all the people on the list the same ethnicity as you? Are they all the same socioeconomic status as you? The list could indicate that you are very family oriented, or very connected to your church community or your neighborhood. Who is missing from this list that you wish was on it? Think of three ways you can stretch yourself in relationships this year. Perhaps make a commitment to get to know a new family in your neighborhood, village, or town, to befriend a family from a different ethnic group in your church, or simply to reach out to a family member you've become distant from. Put this commitment into your action plan.

_____

_____

_____

Prayer

Lord, help me to remember that your heart is for the people, not just the cause. Give me a tender heart toward those experiencing injustice; keep me from apathy. As I passionately seek justice, help me to not do so at the expense of my family and friends, but may my pursuit of justice bring my entire community closer to you.

Justice and Creation Care: A vision for all creation to flourish!

"Tackling the issue of climate change presents us with an inflection point in human history—a climate justice revolution that separates development from fossil fuels, supports people in the most vulnerable situations to adapt, allows all people to take part, and, most importantly, realize their full potential." Mary Robinson

"In the words of St. Theresa of Avila, we are God's hands and feet on earth, now is the time for us, rooted in prayer, to step up and take action on the climate crisis." The Most Revd Dr. Thabo Makgoba

"It is not possible to love an unseen God while mistreating God's visible creation." John Woolman

Definitions

Creation Care: Active concern for the environment and work to restore it, both for positive impact on the natural world, and positive impact on humanity.

Climate Change: Long-term changes to the earth's climate, including rising temperatures, more floods, more droughts, and less reliable rainfall, mainly caused by human activity.

Restorative Economy: A vision for life-giving economic and social structures, where all of society is engaged in living within the planet's resources, keeping inequality within reasonable levels and where everybody has their basic needs met.

All Creation

One of the greatest lies of our modern era is that our flourishing and the flourishing of the rest of creation are in competition with one another, but scripture and science tell a very different story. From the shalom of the garden to the renewed earth of Revelation 21, scripture displays a vision for our world where all of God's creation flourishes.

To help demonstrate just how intertwined our fates are, imagine for a minute a world without trees. In the last 12,000 years we've cleared around half of the world's 5.8 trillion trees. Of course this scenario of tree extinction is not a real threat, but this scenario is simply to demonstrate the point.

If every single tree disappeared tomorrow, certainly our world would be less beautiful and majestic, but we'd survive, right? Wrong. If trees were extinct, we would see a mass extinction of humans, animals, and all marine life except for jellyfish.

- Trees are like a pump—they soak up water from the soil and deposit it into the atmosphere as water vapor ... slowly, all cloud formation and rain would stop.

- The earth would become so dry that large swathes of land would begin to fall into the ocean.

- The air would become so polluted that large numbers of people, animals, and other organisms would begin to die off simply from toxicity.

- As the earth heats up in this new tree-less world, the oceans would soon become so acidic that they would kill off all marine life except jellyfish, which might be able to withstand the acidic waters.

- Eventually all water would become unsuitable for consumption and there would be a final wave of mass extinction.

Of course this awful scenario isn't about to happen, but it just shows how intricate, and frankly, gorgeous the design of our world is. God made this world to be interconnected for a reason—and he calls us to care for it not only for creation's sake but also for our own.

A Restorative Economy: For the love of all creation,
by Naomi Foxwood

From the beginning, God's intention for peace in creation (shalom) meant much more than just the absence of violence. Central to a Christian understanding of God's intention for his creation is the idea that life is inherently about intertwined relationships and relatedness. Millennia before the emergence of modern ideas of symbiosis, ecology, or complex adaptive systems, the creation account of the Bible centers on wholeness, the fundamental unity of all of God's creation. As theologian Margaret Barker writes:

"The biblical world view is a vision of the unity of all things, and how the visible material world relates to another dimension of existence that unites all things into one divinely ordained system known as the eternal covenant, the creation covenant."

This is a worldview that stands in marked contrast to the materialist approach to creation that is one of the defining hallmarks of modernity. Far from a prevailing cultural practice of dominating the earth for material gain, the Christian worldview on creation starts from a universe that is radically alive and precious. In this universe, humans have a unique role that encompasses, but also goes far beyond stewardship.

God's intention for creation includes a powerful emphasis on humans' role to show steadfast love for God and each other, and care for God's creation as part of an interconnected set of shalom relationships.

When our relationship with creation is broken, it has a devastating impact on all of our relationships. We're living at a time when the strain on creation is greater than ever before. This is a result of unsustainable development, unbridled consumption, and environmental degradation. This is a violation of God's intention for creation, but it's also taking a toll on people, particularly the most vulnerable among us. It's a special challenge for our generation. In the last 25 years, more people have escaped poverty than at any other time in history because the world economy has grown—but the way we've done it is unsustainable. We've changed the climate and damaged the environment, and if nothing changes, this will push millions of people back into poverty.

Scientists tell us that if the average global temperature rises by more than 1.5 degrees, compared with pre-industrial levels, the consequences could be disastrous. The rise in temperature may not sound very large, but it has a huge impact on lower-income countries, which already face huge development challenges. Some of the current and future impacts of climate change include:

- Unpredictable rainfall: many regions are experiencing huge variations in rainfall, leading to droughts, floods, and crop failures;

- Extreme weather events: heatwaves, floods, and droughts are increasing in intensity and frequency, leading to an increased number of disasters;

- Sea-level rise: as the oceans warm, water expands, leading to rises in the sea level. There is also the threat of polar ice caps melting, leading to an even more dramatic sea-level rise. This threatens low-lying islands and coastal zones;

- Other impacts include increased migration to urban areas, conflicts over food and water and increases in diseases like malaria. Climate change will also have a huge impact on plant and animal biodiversity.

We need an economy that restores and safeguards God's covenant of peace; a restorative economy rather than a destructive economy. In Leviticus, we find the biblical concept of Jubilee: a story that provides us with hope and inspiration for how God's people can live in right relationship with him, with each other, and with the land:

Firstly, Jubilee speaks of environmental restoration. In practice this would mean us living within environmental limits, ensuring that our economy works with, rather than against, the creation that God has given us. In keeping with Psalm 24, the abundance of the earth belongs to all of us, and ultimately to God. That comes with responsibilities both to steward it carefully, but also to share the proceeds of that natural wealth fairly, just as jubilees reset land ownership on an equal per capita basis. Secondly, Jubilee speaks of rest for those living in poverty. A restorative economy would ensure that everyone was able to meet their basic needs, providing an enabling environment and basic floor of economic security and protection to each and every one of the world's 7 billion people. It would offer a foundation for human flourishing and all people being able to realize their potential.

Finally, Jubilee proclaims the need for fair allocation of wealth. A restorative economy would keep inequality within reasonable limits. This does not just include income inequality, but also unequal benefit from the natural wealth of the land which is our shared inheritance.

Many of the changes needed to respond to our environmental crisis and related humanitarian crises involve sacrifice—but also, paradoxically, offer us the chance to live more fully. They require us to reject conformity with the lifestyle patterns around us and blaze a new trail.

If we do things differently, everyone could have enough to flourish. The Church is called to lead by living simply, thinking differently, and speaking out. If we leave it to the next generation, it'll be too late.

Read Genesis 1 Together
The Beginning

1 In the beginning God created the heavens and the earth.

2 Now the earth was formless and empty, darkness was over the surface of the deep, and the Spirit of God was hovering over the waters.

3 And God said, "Let there be light," and there was light.

4 God saw that the light was good, and he separated the light from the darkness.

5 God called the light "day," and the darkness he called "night." And there was evening, and there was morning - the first day.

6 And God said, "Let there be a vault between the waters to separate water from water."

7 So God made the vault and separated the water under the vault from the water above it. And it was so.

8 God called the vault "sky." And there was evening, and there was morning - the second day.

9 And God said, "Let the water under the sky be gathered to one place, and let dry ground appear." And it was so.

10 God called the dry ground "land," and the gathered waters he called "seas." And God saw that it was good.

11 Then God said, "Let the land produce vegetation: seed-bearing plants and trees on the land that bear fruit with seed in it, according to their various kinds." And it was so.

12 The land produced vegetation: plants bearing seed according to their kinds and trees bearing fruit with seed in it according to their kinds. And God saw that it was good.

13 And there was evening, and there was morning - the third day.

14 And God said, "Let there be lights in the vault of the sky to separate the day from the night, and let them serve as signs to mark sacred times, and days and years,

15 and let them be lights in the vault of the sky to give light on the earth." And it was so.

16 God made two great lights - the greater light to govern the day and the lesser light to govern the night. He also made the stars.

17 God set them in the vault of the sky to give light on the earth,

18 to govern the day and the night, and to separate light from darkness. And God saw that it was good.

19 And there was evening, and there was morning - the fourth day.

20 And God said, "Let the water teem with living creatures, and let birds fly above the earth across the vault of the sky."

21 So God created the great creatures of the sea and every living thing with which the water teems and that moves about in it, according to their kinds, and every winged bird according to its kind. And God saw that it was good.

22 God blessed them and said, "Be fruitful and increase in number and fill the water in the seas, and let the birds increase on the earth."

23 And there was evening, and there was morning - the fifth day.

24 And God said, "Let the land produce living creatures according to their kinds: the livestock, the creatures that move along the ground, and the wild animals, each according to its kind." And it was so.

25 God made the wild animals according to their kinds, the livestock according to their kinds, and all the creatures that move along the ground according to their kinds. And God saw that it was good.

26 Then God said, "Let us make mankind in our image, in our likeness, so that they may rule over the fish in the sea and the birds in the sky, over the livestock and all the wild animals, and over all the creatures that move along the ground."

27 So God created mankind in his own image, in the image of God he created them; male and female he created them.

28 God blessed them and said to them, "Be fruitful and increase in number; fill the earth and subdue it. Rule over the fish in the sea and the birds in the sky and over every living creature that moves on the ground.

29 Then God said, "I give you every seed-bearing plant on the face of the whole earth and every tree that has fruit with seed in it. They will be yours for food.

30 And to all the beasts of the earth and all the birds in the sky and all the creatures that move along the ground - everything that has the breath of life in it - I give every green plant for food." And it was so.

31 God saw all that he had made, and it was very good. And there was evening, and there was morning - the sixth day.

Read Genesis 2:1-15 Together

1 Thus the heavens and the earth were completed in all their vast array.

2 By the seventh day God had finished the work he had been doing; so on the seventh day he rested from all his work.

3 Then God blessed the seventh day and made it holy, because on it he rested from all the work of creating that he had done. Adam and Eve

4 This is the account of the heavens and the earth when they were created, when the Lord God made the earth and the heavens.

5 Now no shrub had yet appeared on the earth and no plant had yet sprung up, for the Lord God had not sent rain on the earth and there was no one to work the ground,

6 but streams came up from the earth and watered the whole surface of the ground.

7 Then the Lord God formed a man from the dust of the ground and breathed into his nostrils the breath of life, and the man became a living being.

8 Now the Lord God had planted a garden in the east, in Eden; and there he put the man he had formed.

9 The Lord God made all kinds of trees grow out of the ground - trees that were pleasing to the eye and good for food. In the middle of the garden were the tree of life and the tree of the knowledge of good and evil.

10 A river watering the garden flowed from Eden; from there it was separated into four headwaters.

11 The name of the first is the Pishon; it winds through the entire land of Havilah, where there is gold.

12 (The gold of that land is good; aromatic resin and onyx are also there.)

13 The name of the second river is the Gihon; it winds through the entire land of Cush. 14 The name of the third river is the Tigris; it runs along the east side of Ashur. And the fourth river is the Euphrates.

15 The Lord God took the man and put him in the Garden of Eden to work it and take care of it.

Questions for Discussion

1. What is the clearest connection you see between brokenness in the environment and brokenness in humanity?

   _____

   _____

   _____

2. What is your theology of creation care? Do you have one?

   _____

   _____

   _____

3. What are some of the ways you try to care for God's creation in your daily life?

   _____

   _____

   _____

4. Why do you think the church historically has been largely silent on care of creation? Do you think this is changing?

   _____

   _____

   _____

5. What is God saying to you, and what are you going to do about it?

   _____

   _____

   _____

   _____

Together

Take a moment and write down three justice issues you are most passionate about. There is no "right" answer here: create a list of what's on your heart, whether that be refugees, racism, conflict, hunger, human trafficking, extreme poverty, or climate change. Share your list with each other, and write down the three issues that get mentioned the most. Now, as a group, discuss how creation care (or the lack of creation care) impacts those issues. This will help show the relationship between the environment and what we typically think of as humanitarian issues.

Let's take racial justice for example:

- African-Americans are exposed to 56% more air pollution than they produce, while white Americans are exposed to only 17% of the air pollution they produce.

- This disparity in air quality has deeply impacted African-American children who are five times more likely than white children to have asthma.

- This disparity isn't by accident: Historically, landfills, industrial sites, toxic and hazardous waste disposal sites have by design been placed in or near communities of color.

Begin learning together how care for creation and care for people are intertwined.

Solo Work

Examine the actions you take in a week that may impact the environment. Look at your lifestyle and the decisions you make that depend on God's creation: consumption of resources, food, waste, etc. Add a "creation care" piece to your action plan. Think of three things you can begin to change about your regular habits that will have a positive impact on creation.

Prayer

Lord, forgive me for actions I have taken that harm your creation. Please guide me to be more aware of protecting the world you have made. Help me see how the actions I take affect your creation and my brothers and sisters around the world. Guide my decisions to live in shalom with all of creation.

How Shall We Live? A lifestyle of justice

"Jesus came to bring complete transformation in us – transformation of our lives ... to bring justice into this world." Kuki Rokhum

"The fruit of justice will be peace" Réne Padilla

Justice is not a project,
by Jason Fileta

Over the last few years I've seen greater and greater acceptance from Christians using the word "justice" to describe ministry. I recall a time when justice was considered too radical to discuss, but now even the most colonial mission trip will be marketed as a "justice trip". Though I rejoice in less fear around this word, I think we often misuse it.

Our models of engaging justice have often been influenced more by our culture than by Scripture and the Spirit. We have made the gospel so bare that somehow it is possible to believe it, to live by it and to accept it while remaining neutral to injustice, absent from the care of creation, and isolated from the poor and vulnerable. To supplement this scarce meal; we have made pursuing justice for the poor and oppressed a side dish. Justice as a project.

Domesticated love makes justice a project.

I am the first to admit that those who have perpetuated "justice as a project" the most are people like me, who work in Christian NGOs whose entire purpose is to alleviate suffering and to respond to injustice. We made justice a project because it is easier to market it that way. We have inspired people with Scripture and with stories of injustice and of hope and transformation. We have prayed mightily for apathy to end. And then, after we have stirred people's souls and inspired folks to join our movements, we have asked people to subcontract the project to us. **We have created a system built on both conviction and convenience.** We want justice to be a commodity that we can sell you on Amazon, and like the other products you buy it must have a low barrier to entry, low cost, and low demand on you. We do not want to interrupt comfort and convenience, we just want to share in the benefits...and this has worked well enough to perpetuate the model.

There is no doubt that good work has happened. God has used our meagre offerings, and God has transformed communities. Some slaves have been set free, some chains have been broken, and some hungry have been fed. But it is not enough. It is a grave mistake for those of us who work in the field of international justice to mobilize our supporters in such a way as to encourage them to maintain lifestyles sustained by the oppression of others as long as they tithe 10 percent. This framework must be challenged.

It is time to be honest: our response to poverty, injustice, and a creation that is groaning cannot be contained to once-a-year giving or a 10 percent threshold. It may be cheap, accessible, and easy in one sense, but it is highway robbery to the fullness of what it means to follow Jesus in an unjust world. It cheapens the call to discipleship not just because it impacts our world deeply, but also because it robs us of a deeply meaningful relationship with our brothers and sisters around the world. It prevents us from wrestling with difficult questions and working out our faith with fear and trembling, and from having to live radically. Domesticated love creates just enough good to keep us from wholeheartedly rejecting evil.

Justice as a project is not only cheapening the experience of those of us who feel the conviction to fight injustice, but it is really not doing the good it could be doing in the field around the world. We cannot continue with this model.

We have seen the fruit of this model in North America. The fruit of this model has been that so many of my friends have walked away from their faith because it did not seem like it was worth sticking around for. So many people have been burdened by a world filled with poverty, racism, injustice, and environmental degradation, and have somehow come to believe that following

Jesus says nothing about this burden. **We made it possible to follow Jesus and have nothing to say about injustice.** Domesticated love with justice as a project is not enough.

Justice as a project allows us to draw a red X for anti-slavery on one hand and then purchase goods made by slaves with our other hand.

Justice as a project allows us to vote for politicians and celebrate policies that completely devastate the environment and perpetuate climate change, but then quickly give money to support the children of impoverished farmers no longer able to grow food because of our climate crisis.

Justice as a project allows us to mobilize blankets and backpacks of supplies for people who are fleeing conflict as refugees, but then also celebrate when our government closes the door to admitting refugees into our own nation.

Justice as a project allows us to mobilize resources for African communities facing crisis and remain silent when African Americans are being murdered by police.

These are the fruits of justice as a project – it is very incomplete. Things ostensibly done to benefit others are often designed around what would most benefit us. This is a far cry from radical discipleship.

We have taken the ocean of sin that infects our world, and reduced immense evil to simple questions of personal piety. Our notions of sin have been so personal that our idea of redemption is similarly so personal. We have failed to see the sins of systems, of culture, of nations. Therefore, we do not think God's redemption has to touch those things. This is the beauty of our God – the God who is so deeply concerned with the slavery of God's people in Egypt is also deeply concerned with my small life. Sin is both personal and systemic, and so are the reaches of God's redemption.

We must look to the life of Christ to escape this paradigm of domesticated love, and instead love relentlessly. Relentless love integrates justice into every aspect of life. Jesus' love always led to action. I wish we could make that part of the terms of service of Twitter–that we would never be deceived enough to believe that our words are enough. It is a system of convenience that produces activism that is measured by likes and retweets rather than policy or behavior change. This is markedly different than the deep compassion Jesus had that always found action.

We must rely on God's power, not on our performance or activities. Awakenings to the implications of whole-life discipleship – the relentless love and lifestyle of justice – are often accompanied quickly by burnout, disillusionment, and disappointment. To avoid this, it is critical to always remember two things: that we will not save the world, and that God IS saving and redeeming all things!

I have found prayer to be the most important anchor for me to remember that I am not God, allowing those burdens that are only for him to remain with him, but also stay focused on my calling as Jesus's disciple. I have also found myself coming back again and again to the promise of God in Revelation 21, that one day when Jesus reigns there will be no more suffering, no more death, no more racism, no more poverty, no more injustice.

All things will be made new, even the rest of creation. The evangelistic implications of this have surprised me – more often than not I find myself preaching the gospel and declaring who God is when I am declaring how things were meant to be, and one day will be. When we look at a world and see injustice it is an opportunity to say that God never intended it to be this way. Every denouncing of injustice is an opportunity to announce the character, promises and goodness of God.

Together

This week, instead of reading scripture together, you will present your action plans to each other. Offer feedback and come up with ways to hold each other accountable (e.g., accountability partners, sending text messages or emails at the beginning of each month or setting aside time once a month to check on each other's progress, etc).

Most importantly we encourage you to reflect on the study and for one last time ask "What is

God saying to you, and what are you going to do about it?" Feel free as well to share your creative expression with each other.

Spend time in prayer. Pray for each other, pray for your communities, for our nation and for our world. Pray for God's spirit to walk with you as you continue to live justly.

Finally, some groups may choose to fill out the Church Justice Evaluation[5] and examine how your church community is engaging with justice — this might be a great activity to help you identify the ways you could begin to influence your broader church community.

Solo Work

Edit your plans based upon the feedback you received from your group. Review some of the plans you made early on in the study. Perhaps your perspective has changed on certain things? We would love to see a copy of your action plan -- you can send us your action plan at livejustly@tearfundusa.org

Prayer

Lord, forgive me for the times I forsake your mission in the world for my own comfort. Guide me as I put this plan of daily justice into action. Help it not to be a checklist I seek to complete each day, but let it come from an attitude of worship. Give me the endurance, desire and will to allow justice to truly encompass my actions. Help me to be a person who lives justly. Help me to be more like Jesus.

---

5 You can find the Church Justice Evaluation on page 87

Part Three

Resources

Micah Declaration on Integral Mission

The Micah Network (now Micah Global) is a coalition of evangelical churches and agencies from around the world that are committed to integral mission. In 2001, One hundred and forty Christians from 50 countries gathered in Oxford to discuss the challenges facing our world. Some of the language is dated or not up to our current communication standards, but we left it as is because it is a historical document from a time and place. It is inspiring and inspired.

This document has been foundational for so many in the Global South as they work to overcome poverty and injustice in their communities, but it has never been widely read by Christians in the Global North.

INTEGRAL MISSION

Integral mission, or holistic transformation, is the proclamation and demonstration of the Gospel. It is not simply that evangelism and social involvement are to be done alongside each other, rather, in integral mission, our proclamation has social consequences as we call people to love and repentance in all areas of life. Our social involvement has evangelistic consequences as we bear witness to the transforming grace of Jesus Christ.

If we ignore the world, we betray the word of God, which sends us out to serve the world. If we ignore the word of God, we have nothing to bring to the world. Justice and justification by faith, worship and political action, the spiritual and the material, personal change and structural change all belong together. As in the life of Jesus, being, doing, and saying are at the heart of our integral task.

We call one another back to the centrality of Jesus Christ. His life of sacrificial service is the pattern for Christian discipleship. In his life and through his death, Jesus modeled identification with the poor and inclusion of the other. On the cross, God shows us how seriously he takes justice, reconciling both rich and poor to himself as he meets the demands of his justice. We serve by the power of the risen Lord through the Spirit as we journey with the poor, finding our hope in the subjection of all things under Christ and the final defeat of evil. We confess that all too often we have failed to live a life worthy of this gospel.

The grace of God is the heartbeat of integral mission. As recipients of undeserved love we are to show grace, generosity and inclusiveness. Grace redefines justice as, not merely honouring a contract, but helping the disadvantaged.

INTEGRAL MISSION WITH THE POOR AND MARGINALIZED

The poor, like everyone else, bear the image of the Creator. They have knowledge, abilities and resources. Treating the poor with respect means enabling the poor to be the architects of change in their communities, rather than imposing solutions upon them. Working with the poor involves building relationships that lead to mutual change. We welcome welfare activities as important in serving with the poor. Welfare activities, however, must be extended to include movement toward value transformation, the empowerment of communities, and cooperation in wider issues of justice. Because of its presence among the poor, the Church is in a unique position to restore their God-given dignity by enabling them to produce their own resources and to create solidarity networks.

We object to any use of the word "development" that implies some countries are civilized and developed, while others are uncivilised and under-developed. This imposes a narrow and linear economic model of development, and fails to recognize the need for transformation in so-called "developed" countries. While we recognize the value of planning, organization, evaluation and other such tools, we believe they must be subservient to the process of building relationships, changing values, and empowering the poor.

Work with the poor involves setbacks, opposition, and suffering. But we have also been inspired and encouraged by stories of change. In the midst of hopelessness we have hope.

INTEGRAL MISSION AND THE CHURCH

God by his grace has given local churches the task of integral mission. The future of integral mission is in planting and enabling local churches to transform the communities of which they are part. Churches, as caring and inclusive communities, are at the heart of what it means to do integral mission. People are often attracted to the Christian community before they are attracted to the Christian message.

Our experience of walking with poor communities challenges our concept of what it means to be a church. The Church is not merely an institution or organization, but a community of Jesus that embodies the values of the Kingdom. The involvement of the poor in the life of the church is forcing us to find new ways of being church within the context of our cultures instead of being mere reflections of the values of one dominant culture or sub-culture. Our message has credibility to the extent that we adopt an incarnational approach. We confess that too often the church has pursued wealth, success, status, and influence. But the kingdom of God has been given to the community that Jesus Christ called his little flock.

We do not want our church traditions to hinder working together for the sake of the Kingdom. We need one another. The church can best address poverty by working with the poor and other stakeholders like civil society, government, and the private sector. In these relationships, mutual respect, and a recognition of the distinctive role of each partner must be observed.

We offer the Micah Network as one opportunity for collaboration for the sake of the poor and the Gospel.

INTEGRAL MISSION AND ADVOCACY

We confess that, in a world of conflict and ethnic tension, we have often failed to build bridges. We are called to work for reconciliation between ethnically divided communities, between rich and poor, and between the oppressors and the oppressed.

We acknowledge the command to speak up for those who cannot speak for themselves, for the rights of all who are destitute in a world that has given "money rights" greater priority than human rights. We recognize the need for advocacy both to address structural injustice and to rescue needy neighbours.

Globalization is often, in reality, the dominance of cultures that have the power to project their goods, technologies, and images far beyond their borders. In the face of this, the Church in its rich diversity has a unique role as a truly global community. We exhort Christians to network and cooperate to face together the challenges of globalization. The Church needs a unified global voice to respond to the damage caused by it to both human beings and the environment. Our hope for the Micah Network is that it will foster a movement of resistance to a global system of exploitation.

We affirm that the struggle against injustice is spiritual. We commit ourselves to prayer, advocating on behalf of the poor, not only before the rulers of this world, but also before the Judge of all nations.

INTEGRAL MISSION AND LIFESTYLE

Integral mission is the concern of every Christian. We want to see the poor through the eyes of Jesus, who, as he looked on the crowds, had compassion on them because they were harassed and helpless like sheep without a shepherd.

There is a need for integral discipleship involving the responsible and sustainable use of the resources of God's creation, and the transformation of the moral, intellectual, economic, cultural, and political dimensions of our lives. For many of us, this includes reviving a biblical sense of stewardship. The concept of Sabbath reminds us that there should be limits to our consumption.

Wealthy Christians, both in the West and in the Two-Thirds World, must use their wealth in the service of others. We are committed to the liberation of the rich from slavery to money and power. The hope of treasure in heaven releases us from the tyranny of mammon.

Our prayer is that, in our day and in our different contexts, we may be able to do what the Lord requires of us: to act justly, to love mercy, and to walk humbly with our God.

27 September 2001

Long Term action Plan

ACTION	TIMEFRAME	NOTES
Sample: Pray for racial justice	Once per day for a year	I'm going to write my prayers down in a journal

ACTION	TIMEFRAME	NOTES

Advocacy for Justice: A look at poverty-focused development assistance

Often when we think of prophetic political advocacy, we picture times when brave men and women of faith have stood up to injustice—William Wilberforce ending the transatlantic slave trade, Dr. King fighting against segregation, and the Jubilee movement to cancel odious debts. **Sometimes, however, our role as prophetic advocates is to push our leaders to maintain and expand just policies that cultivate flourishing communities!**

Poverty-focused development assistance (PFDA) is a catch-all term describing any foreign assistance given by the U.S. government for the express purpose of poverty alleviation. This helps distinguish it from foreign assistance used for political or military purposes. **The effect of PFDA is astounding and something that we as citizens should be proud of and fight to protect!**

For less than 1% of the federal budget, PFDA is transforming lives and communities around the world!

THE FACTS

Because of poverty-focused development assistance:

- 6.7 million people living with HIV/AIDS receive life-saving anti-retroviral medication.
- More than 22 million children are enrolled in USAID-funded schools.
- Three million children's lives are saved every year through USAID immunization programs.
- 8.8 million children under the age of five have been reached by nutrition programs.

Another aspect of PFDA we applaud is the role of trusted Christian organizations in implementing assistance. Organizations such as Tearfund, World Vision, Food for the Hungry, World Relief, and many others have received over $1,000,000,000 (yep, that's $1 billion!) in the last five years alone to do the incredible lifesaving work of providing vaccines, delivering food, providing bed nets to protect against malaria, providing agricultural training, etc.

Here's the thing—this funding is always at risk of being dramatically decreased. Our leaders won't continue to fund programs like these if they don't know where we (the voters) stand. It's time to speak out and encourage our leaders to keep PFDA well-funded!

Call script for session five

STEPS TO CALLING CONGRESS WITH YOUR GROUP

1. Log onto house.gov and type in your ZIP code to see who represents you in the House of Representatives.

2. Call the capitol switchboard at 202-224-3121. They are there 24 hours a day and will forward your call to your member's office.

3. Leave a message either with the staffer who answers the phone or on the machine:

SAMPLE MESSAGE

"Hi, this is **<<Your Name>>**, a constituent from **<<Your City>>**. I'm doing a small group study with my church, **<<Your Church name>>**, on justice. We've just finished learning about the incredible ways foreign assistance has helped people living in extreme poverty. We want to urge Representative **<<Your Member's Name>>** to be a champion of poverty-focused development assistance. For less than 1% of the federal budget, lives are being saved and communities transformed. ***If leaving a message*** We'd love to hear back from you regarding this important issue. Please call me back at **<<Your Number>>**. Thank you for your time and your service. We are praying for you."

SOME TIPS FOR YOUR PHONE CALL

• Feel free to make it personal: talk about why you care about people living in extreme poverty.

• You will be educating them—they probably know less about poverty-focused development assistance than you do!

• You are calling on a general issue that will always be relevant, not on a specific bill. Budget negotiations are ongoing, and it never hurts to let a member of Congress know where you stand—with people in extreme poverty!

• Don't be afraid of your faith! If you are in a conversation, feel free to let them know that your faith compels you to stand with the impoverished!

Church Justice Evaluation

The Spirit is moving and inspiring churches around the country to seek justice. Throughout our neighborhoods, cities, and even the world Christians are standing with the vulnerable in the face of oppression and injustice. They are speaking out on issues of extreme poverty, HIV/AIDS, immigration, corruption, racial inequality, and more. **We praise God for this movement of the Spirit, and long to see a church standing for justice become the norm rather than the exception.**

But, how do we measure our progress in the direction of justice? In which areas of justice is our community strong, and in which areas do we need to improve? Where are we simply paying lip service to justice, and where are we actively seeking justice?

These are the questions we hope to help you answer using this Church Justice Evaluation. **The Church Justice Evaluation (CJE) is designed to help you discover your church's baseline attitudes and behaviors related to justice**. It is our hope and prayer that every year you revisit the CJE and that each year you see the needle move towards more informed theology surrounding justice and practical action for justice!

Some churches have a deep and documented history in aligning themselves with justice work like churches seeking equality and fairness under the law like many African American churches during the Civil Rights Movement, and some churches are just now discovering their commitment to justice as they explore issues like human trafficking and clean water initiatives. No matter where your church stands, the CJE is a tool to help you evaluate your church's attitudes and behaviors related to justice in six key areas:

- **Justice and Advocacy**
- **Justice and Prayer**
- **Justice and Consumption**
- **Justice and Generosity**
- **Justice and Relationships**
- **Justice and Creation Care**

This evaluation is by no means comprehensive, but is a useful tool to help you identify and celebrate your strengths and improve upon your weaknesses. **As a global organization working for justice in 50 countries we wrote the CJE through a global lens, but hope it illuminates not only your commitment to global justice, but opportunities for local justice as well.**

Step 1: Evaluate

Answer questions, scoring your congregation on a scale of 1–5 for each question. There are 8-10 questions measuring attitudes and 8-10 questions measuring behavior for each of the areas of evaluation. The scale is a likert scale where:

1 — Strongly Disagree
2 — Disagree
3 — Neutral
4 — Agree
5 — Strongly Agree

Step 2: Reflect

The scores will help you identify the areas of greatest strength and where there is room for growth in your church's response to injustice.

We understand that your church will not score high in all areas. In fact, it's okay if your church scores low in each category. Just by taking time to evaluate your church, you've shown an interest and level of commitment to justice that is needed in the global church.

Take time to reflect on each of your scores and seek out the opportunities for growth that are outlined at the end of the CJE. Meet with church leaders and make plans to implement new strategies based upon what you have learned.

Step 3: Grow and Celebrate

The scores will help you identify the areas of greatest strength and where there is room for growth in your The church group filling out the evaluation will set targets for growth and celebration to be implemented in the following year. Share these with your church's leadership!

Tearfund is committed to walking with you and your church to seek justice. A wonderful next step is to use Live Justly with your churches small groups. **We mean it when we say we want to journey with you—please get in touch with our team and let us know how we can support your journey to live justly as a church!**

Justice and Advocacy

"Speak out for justice! Stand up for the poor and destitute!" Proverbs 31:9b

In the biblical tradition of Moses, Esther, and Jesus we ought to challenge structures and systems—not with anger or violence, but educated and informed advocacy.

Many of us, if we are to be honest, do not engage with politics. In fact, we might avoid them altogether. Political matters are oftentimes confusing, complicated, and can leave us with a sense of hopelessness, wondering if we can even make a significant difference at the systemic level. The truth, however, is that as followers of Jesus we are summoned to actively challenge unjust laws and political structures that perpetuate injustice as well as reinforce those policies that promote flourishing.

As the Church, we must not ignore the legal systems and economic structures that keep our brothers and sisters trapped in extreme poverty. We are instructed to speak up and fight for those who have had their voices taken away. If the church does not work together to dismantle unjust systems and usher in God's Kingdom, who will?

1. People in my Church are actively engaged in changing policies that perpetuate injustice.

2. My Church regularly (4x/year) provides opportunities to influence public policy for more just outcomes.

3. My church has a team or small group that actively seeks to influence public policy on behalf of the marginalized and oppressed.

4. In the last 6 months my Church has provided an opportunity in a worship service for people to take an advocacy action (sign a petition, sign postcards to elected officials, etc.)

1 Strongly Disagree   2 Disagree   3 Neutral   4 Agree   5 Strongly Agree

5. When my church engages with marginalized people we also take time to understand the systemic causes of their condition. (e.g. The Church homeless outreach also studies affordable housing policy)

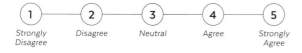

1 Strongly Disagree   2 Disagree   3 Neutral   4 Agree   5 Strongly Agree

6. My church leadership regularly signs (4x/year) letters or statements aimed at holding elected officials accountable to just policies.

1 Strongly Disagree   2 Disagree   3 Neutral   4 Agree   5 Strongly Agree

7. My church regularly (4x/year) has had teaching/preaching that touches on the role Christians can play in securing justice through advocacy.

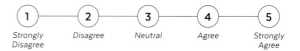

1 Strongly Disagree   2 Disagree   3 Neutral   4 Agree   5 Strongly Agree

8. My church financially supports ministries that seek to change policy in order to secure justice for the marginalized and oppressed.

1 Strongly Disagree   2 Disagree   3 Neutral   4 Agree   5 Strongly Agree

9. My church has organized a visit with our local or nationally elected officials regarding a policy that impacts the marginalized in our own community or our world.

1 Strongly Disagree   2 Disagree   3 Neutral   4 Agree   5 Strongly Agree

Score: ___ /45

1. People at my church view public policy advocacy, campaigning, and social action **to** secure justice as Kingdom work.

2. My church understands the roles policy **plays** in securing justice and promoting human flourishing.

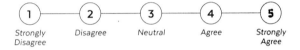

3. The people in my church understand that issues like hunger, poverty, etc. cannot be solved solely through direct service but **require** systemic change.

4. When my church refers to biblical justice we are usually referring to social and economic justice, not to God's judgement.

5. My church believes it is important to hold elected officials accountable to standards of justice.

6. People in my church admire people like William Wilberforce, Dr. Martin Luther King Jr., and Nelson Mandela who advanced the Kingdom through struggle and policy change and want to do the same.

7. My church believes that justice and concern for the marginalized and oppressed is central to God's character.

8. My church believes that to be a Christian and not seek justice is to miss an essential component of following Christ.

Score: ___ /40

Justice and Advocacy score summary

| Behavior: ___ /45 | Attitude: ___ /40 |

Justice and Prayer

"They Kingdom come, thy will be done on earth as it is in Heaven...:"

"The power of prayer" is a phrase we hear often. Indeed we know and believe that prayer changes things, but how often do we actually pray in such a way that reflects that belief? We look at the brokenness throughout the world and feel the urge to do something about it. We try to find organizations that are addressing the issues and we get involved, donating our time, energy, and money. But ultimately, challenges such as poverty, hunger, gender inequality, and slavery overwhelm us.

After some time, we begin to wonder if our participation in addressing these issues is actually doing any good, creating any positive change. **It is in these moments that we must remember that we will not be the ones to bring justice into the world, but that God will**. Prayer must become a primary action in seeking justice. As we pray, we are asking God to intercede with his love and sovereignty. As we pray, we give to God what is His to redeem and to reconcile.

BEHAVIOR

1. My Church organizes community prayer times outside of the worship service each week.

2. In the last twelve months our church has regularly (once a month) prayed about situations of poverty and injustice during worship services.

3. My Church regularly (4x/year) prays for elected officials and decision makers to be wise, just, and to protect the weak.

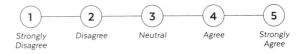

4. When overwhelmed with a situation of injustice my Church's first response is prayer.

7. At least once a year there is teaching dedicated to prayer, and encouraging members to pray.

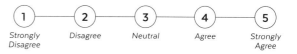

5. Church leadership (lay or ordained) takes the time to inform the congregation of ways they can pray for the church, the city, and the world throughout the week.

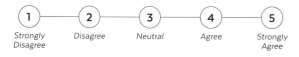

8. Our church prays for miracles in situations where we don't know how else to pray.

Score: ___ /40

6. When major meetings and events happen in our world our church takes time to pray over their outcome (e.g. elections, war, conflict, etc.).

1. My church believes prayer is a central practice of the Christian life.

2. The people in my church have a strong sense that God calls them to pray for impoverished and oppressed communities.

3. Somebody who listened to the prayers offered in our church in the last month (e.g. small groups, prayer chains, congregational prayers) would recognize overcoming poverty and oppression as a regular focus of our church's prayer life.

4. Within our church, prayer does not feel like a chore but rather our opportunity to intimately connect with God.

5. Within our Community we view prayer not only as a means of connecting to God, but to our world.

6. During corporate prayer the Holy Spirit's presence is felt.

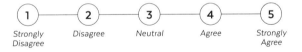

7. Our church believes that God works in our world
    through prayer.

8. People in our Church believe that God changes
    their hearts through prayer.

9. Our church believes that God speaks to us
    through prayer.

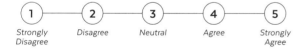

Score: ___ /45

Justice and Prayer score summary

| Behavior: ___ /40 | Attitude: ___ /45 |

Justice and Consumption

"Every dollar you spend . . . or don't spend . . . is a vote you cast for the world you want." L.N. Smith

Everyday, we make choices about what we do or do not consume. Whether or not we acknowledge it, our consumption habits have a significant impact, for better or for worse, on people around the world. From the coffee or tea we drink to the clothing items we buy, behind each purchase is the work of a person. These people have hopes, dreams, and ambitions, but far too many of them are unable to freely pursue such aspirations because they are trapped working in unethical working conditions with inadequate living wages.

Many companies producing the goods available to us seek the highest profit, sacrificing the livelihood of workers in the process. **As ordinary consumers, we have extraordinary power to change this.** We have the ability to say that we care more about the individuals, than the product itself. We can do so by becoming educated and aware about how our products are made and then making decisions in a way that demands people be treated with dignity. People matter and are invaluable, not to be used as commodities. **May our choices of consumption begin to reflect that and may we, as the Church, make decisions that value people above product.**

BEHAVIOR

1. People in my church are active in reducing their consumption so they are able to share more with the impoverished.

2. People in my church ensure they are consuming in ways that are environmentally friendly.

3. People in my church recycle goods among each other so as to avoid increased consumption.

4. Our church has implemented a plan to consume resources in an environmentally sensitive way and to use fair trade supplies.

7. My church teaches about simplicity, and about avoiding consumerism as a spiritual discipline.

5. People in my church research the products they buy, in order to ensure the products they purchase are not harmful to people or the environment.

8. My church regularly (2x/year) encourages members to donate unused/unnecessary items to charity.

Score: ___ /40

6. People in my church choose not to buy items from certain companies until they change their policies and practices to be more ethical (no slave labor, pay fair wages, no child labor, more earth friendly practices, abide by safety codes, etc).

1. People in my church have a strong sense that there is a link between consuming justly and discipleship.

2. People in my church are aware that international trade policies and local and international labor laws affect the quality of life for the impoverished around the world.

3. People in my church understand that when you give money to a company (ethical, or not) you are telling them you support their products, choices, and the way they 'do business.'

4. My congregation understands that by choosing what's 'cheap/easy' usually means the cost is borne not by us, but by the producers of good.

5. My church views consumerism as an idol and views simplicity as a true discipline.

6. People in my church desire to seek justice through the use of their finances.

7. My church understands that seeking justice through their purchases is not simply a set of rules, but it is an act of worship to God.

8. My church understands the connection between their purchases and the hands that made them.

Score: ___ /45

Justice and Consumption score summary

Behavior: ___ /40	Attitude: ___ /40

Justice and Generosity

"Philanthropy and generosity are not reserved for the elite. You don't have to be a rockstar, millionaire, or a celebrity to be generous. The root word for philanthropy literally means love of humanity, and this is something we can all do. This is something we must all do. This kind of love can change the world and when we live this simple truth we'll be change ourselves." -Eugene Cho

Money, time, and energy. These are things that we seemingly always want more of. But what if, instead of chasing after such things, we gave of what we already have – shifted our focus from getting to giving? What if we gave out of our substance instead of our abundance? As people living in the western world, we already live with abundance compared to the majority world. We have access to more resources and have greater financial wealth than over 80% of all people. We must use what has been given to us to help our brothers and sisters throughout the world who live with far less.

We are called to be good stewards of the gifts God gives us and everything we have has been given to us. Jesus calls us to live, love, and give sacrificially because he did so for us first. Giving sacrificially is difficult, but with it comes joy and fulfillment that is deep and profound. As image bearers of Christ,

we are to give of ourselves just as he gave to us, for God created us in such a way that generosity towards others would fill our hearts with abounding joy.

BEHAVIOR

1. Our church budget provides for generous contribution to ministries that serve marginalized communities around the world.

2. Our church budget is provides generously to church run ministries that serve marginalized communities locally.

3. In the last twelve months our church actively campaigned to raise support for a ministry that is outside of our church.

4. If someone outside our church looked at our church budget they would identify generosity to the poor as a core value of our church.

5. People in our church give of both their finances and their time to assist those living in poverty.

6. My church has taught on generosity in the last year.

7. Our congregation comes the aid of church members who are in need of financial assistance.

8. Seminars on financial freedom also include instruction on giving and generosity.

Score: ___ /40

1. People in my church have a strong sense that God calls them to be generous toward the poor.

2. People in my church strongly identify with those living in poverty and are filled with compassion when they consider the need of the world's most impoverished.

3. People in my church view their money and possessions with a 'light grip,' meaning they can easily let go of them.

4. People in my congregation love giving, because they know in giving, we receive.

5. Our church embraces giving to causes and needs that are outside of our church family.

6. People in our church understand the importance of being generous with their time to help alleviate all kinds of poverty (financial, physical, emotional, spiritual, etc.)

7. People in our church have an attitude of thanksgiving when we give.

8. Our church views wealth as an opportunity for to be a blessing more than as blessing.

Score: ___ /40

Justice and Generosity score summary

Behavior: ___ /40	Attitude: ___ /40

Justice and Relationships

"Love for God and love for neighbor empower and eradicate the distance between every human being. when we begin to truly comprehend that the word became flesh and walked among us we will have a deeper understanding of humility and self sacrificing love" Sunia Gibbs

We were created to be in relationship; to know and be known. In the hyper-individualistic and success-driven society that we live in, relationships easily get placed on the wayside.We can find ourselves too busy working and striving towards more, rather than investing in our family and friends.**Even if such work is of noble cause, we must not forget about the loved ones God has given us.** He gave us family and friends to experience deep community and love, so that we might grow closer to God and know him more fully.

On the other hand, we also must not get so caught up in the relationships with those most like us that we lose sight of those in need. Working for justice begins with knowing those oppressed by injustice. Walking with them, knowing them, loving them authentically. **Out of authentic relationships we can be spurred to informed action.**

Beautiful and powerful things happen when Christ-like love is the motivation and people are the recipients of such love.

BEHAVIOR

1. People in my church interact and are friends with people who live in the margins of society.

2. My church teaches on self-care for those in ministry.

3. My church provides opportunities to directly engage with the marginalized not as service providers, but as friends.

4. In my church our leaders keep strong boundaries in their own lives to keep from 'burn out.'

5. Our church is geographically positioned so that those living within the margins of society can easily reach us and we can easily reach them.

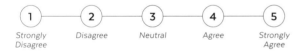

6. Our presence within our neighborhood is so strong that if we moved, people in the community would notice.

7. Our church is ethnically and economically diverse.

8. Individuals who have engaged with our church are treated as beloved and with dignity, not as projects to help us accomplish our goals.

Score: ___ /40

1. My church regularly speaks about maintaining a balance between working, ministry, and maintaining relationships.

4. People in my church strongly identify with the impoverished.

2. People in my church seek to understand people suffering from injustice and not just the facts.

5. The people in my church view the Great Commission and the pursuit of justice to be integrally linked.

3. My church understands that our social engagement has evangelistic consequences.

6. As a church our ministry is heavily influenced by those within the margins of society and those who do not hold traditional power in our world.

7. As a church our theology is heavily influenced by those within the margins of society, and those who do not hold traditional power in our world.

Justice and Relationships score summary

Behavior: ___ /40	Attitude: ___ /45

8. We are challenged and embrace Jesus' example of embracing the outcast in his society.

9. People in our church value diversity.

Score: ___ /45

Justice and Creation Care

"It is not possible to love and unseen God while mistreating God's visible creation." John Woolman

Creation Care is a hotly debated topic today. As Christians, however, caring for creation is a duty and a privilege. God entrusted to us the beautiful earth he created and his intention for the world is to live in harmony and peace with one another. We were created to live in community with all of creation, which includes people, land, animals, and all else that God created.

Despite what many think, our choices of how we live on this earth affect people throughout the world. Individual choices such as modes of transportation, food consumption, and recycling habits have a ripple effect. At the scale that we consume in a modern and highly developed nation, massive changes are happening throughout the globe. Such changes are adversely affecting many countries in the Global South, as they experience crop failures and droughts due to climate change and demand, they are left to struggle for food and water. Living lives of abundance and enjoying the privilege of choice leaves our brothers and sisters to suffer the consequences of such consumption habits.

As we walk upon this earth that God created, may we walk gently, consciously, and compassionately with all of creation.

BEHAVIOR

1. Our church embraces recycling and reuse of goods, and reducing consumption

2. The majority of our church follow the practice recycling and reuse of goods, and reducing consumption in their personal lives.

3. We hold regular events (2x/year) where we help rebuild/repair part of creation (planting trees, cleaning parks, etc.)

4. Our church teaches regularly (4x/year) on the importance of creation care.

5. We organize events like a clothes swap, garage sales, etc. in order to reduce consumption of new goods and filling of landfills

6. Our church has performed an energy audit to understand ways we could be more sustainable.

7. Our church has a committee focused on energy use and sustainability.

8. Our church celebrates creation through camping, backpacking, or other outings exploring God's creation.

9. Our church has a community garden.

Score: ___ /45

1. Most people in our church understand the term 'Creation Care.'

2. Most people in our church feel a responsibility towards creation because of our faith, not as separate from our faith.

3. Our church has an articulated theology of creation care on our website or in other church documents.

4. Our church has engaged learning about complicated issues like climate change rather than dismissing them as political, fabricated or irrelevant.

5. We consider creation care as an integral part of Christian discipline.

6. A visitor to our church would sense that our church has a deep love of God's creation.

7. People in your church have been exposed to the relationship between creation care and poverty.

Score: ___ /35

Justice and Creation Care score summary

| Behavior: ___ /45 | Attitude: ___ /35 |

Alright,
You made it!

Time to add up your total behavior and total
attitude scores! Remember, this score is here
to help you understand your engagement with
justice, not as a tool to feel guilt or shame. Use this
score to spark discussion and brainstorm ways to
improve your engagement with justice.

> **Total Behavior Score:** ___ /250

> **Total Attitude Score:** ___ /250

We'd love your feedback on this tool. Help us
improve it with general comments or questions, or
suggestions for different questions!

info@tearfundusa.org

About Tearfund

Tearfund partners with churches and communities to overcome poverty and injustice.

- We work on the front lines of some of the most urgent needs in the world providing emergency food, shelter and water to refugees facing crisis,

- We work in partnership with local churches to respond to pervasive poverty through sustainable agriculture and economic development,

- And we advocate for justice to local, national and international leaders influencing behavior and policies that harm the poorest in our world.

Our vision is for all people to experience restored relationships that free them from poverty and injustice, enabling them to live transformed lives in healthy communities and reach their God-given potential.

Our mission is to follow Jesus where the need is greatest as we work alongside churches and communities to overcome poverty and injustice.

We have seen the incredible power of churches and communities when they partner to lift themselves out of poverty.

Get in touch with us at:

www.tearfundusa.org

888.789.4660

info@tearfundusa.org

$15.00
ISBN 978-0-578-99694-3
51500>

9 780578 996943